The Glorious Future

What the Bible Teaches about the Last Things

William Macleod

Foreword by Robert McCurley

Scottish Reformed Heritage Publications
2023

Copyright © William Macleod, 2023

All rights reserved.
No part of this book may be reproduced in any form or by any means without the prior written permission from the publisher.

Scripture quotations are taken from the King James Version (KJV).

Cover Picture:
'The Plains of Heaven' by John Martin (1789-1854) is part of a collection of three Last Judgment paintings by Martin: 'The Great Day of His Wrath'; 'The Last Judgment'; and 'The Plains of Heaven'. These are housed in the Tate Gallery, London. Photo © Tate.

ISBN: 978-1-4466-8836-6

Publisher:
Scottish Reformed Heritage Publications
J. W. Keddie
19 Newton Park
Kirkhill
Inverness-shire
IV5 7QB

Printed by Lulu (www.lulu.com)

Contents

	Page
Foreword – Robert D. McCurley	7
Introduction	9
1. Old Testament Teaching	12
2. Death	22
3. Events preceding the Second Coming	35
4. Interpreting the Book of Revelation	49
5. The Jews	61
6. Dispensational Premillennialism	73
7. The Second Coming and Resurrection	85
8. The Judgment	97
9. Hell	111
10. Heaven	124
The Author	137

Foreword

Believers can do what no one else can do: they can see into the future. Meteorologists and financial market analysts repeatedly fail to predict what will happen in the week ahead, while the Christian knows with certainty what will happen far beyond their lifetime. How is this possible? The living and true God, who has preordained the future, has also revealed His plan for the future in the Holy Scriptures. He opens the door to the future and opens the believing eye to behold it.

This serves an important purpose. What we believe about the future informs our understanding of the present. In the Christian life, we are compelled to begin with the end. By setting before our mind's eye the days leading up to the end of history (and beyond), we are enabled to discern the priorities and significance of today. Each successive day builds momentum toward the Last Day, beyond which there are no more days in this present world.

In *The Glorious Future*, William Macleod expounds the Scriptures and delves into what God has revealed about the days to come. He covers the span of biblical teaching from the termination of physical life in this world at death to the eternal state of Heaven and Hell in the world to come. Throughout his treatment, he assesses the various positions held by Bible-believing theologians, seeking to treat them with a fair hand, while subjecting them to the litmus test of Scripture itself. While readers (even Reformed readers) may not share his conclusions at every point, they stand to glean keen insight from the study.

Paul insists on "the doctrine which is according to godliness" (1 Timothy 6:3; cf. Titus 1:1; 2:11-12). As Reformed theologians have long held, theology is the doctrine of living unto God through Christ. This highlights one particularly edifying feature of *The Glorious Future*. Pastor Macleod skilfully applies the truths being expounded, both to matters of godly practice and Christian experience. Believers, therefore, will find the Lord feeding and fattening their souls through their reflective meditations on the truths set before them in this book.

I would commend the book to a wide audience, both the young and old, both new believers and experienced saints. May the Lord own and bless this study to the good of the contemporary church and to generations yet unborn.

Rev. Robert D. McCurley
Greenville Presbyterian Church
Greenville
South Carolina
USA

INTRODUCTION

Introduction

This book looks into the future, and, based on the teaching of Scripture, sets out what will happen. The theological term for this is Eschatology. It is the doctrine of the last things. Some people allow their imagination to lead them into fantastical speculation but theology should always be sober and restrained and based firmly and squarely on what God has clearly revealed in the Bible. In trying to interpret prophecy we must exercise a measure of caution as it is notoriously difficult to interpret.

When Christ came the first time, He took almost everyone by surprise. Although the Jews had the wonderful and detailed prophecies of the Old Testament, and they had clear ideas in their own minds what would happen, it did not turn out as they expected. As one writer puts it, when Christ came the first time they all got it wrong, so, very likely, when Christ returns the second time, they will likely all be wrong too. There will be many surprises. Even the best works of theology will be found to be inaccurate. Some things, however, are clearly revealed in Scripture and we can be sure of these things. In this book we will concentrate on these biblical truths.

Eschatology has to be looked at in two ways. First, there is general eschatology which considers the future of the church and of the world and mankind in general. It describes the events which will take place before Christ returns, and then the end of the world, the judgment, and the eternal state. But there is also individual eschatology, which looks at the future from the perspective of the individual. This involves a person's death, what happens after death, the intermediate state, the resurrection, the final judgment, Heaven and Hell.

Current Views

The teaching of evolution by Charles Darwin (1809-1882), especially as advocated by Thomas Huxley (1825-1895), known as 'Darwin's Bulldog', and its general acceptance within the scientific community, in schools, in the media and in the population in general, has to a large extent undermined faith in God. Naturalistic explanations of the origin of the universe and of man, are treated as fact in Western society today. The so-called 'Big-Bang' theory put forward by a Roman Catholic priest, Georges Lemaitre (1894-1966), is seen as the basic answer to all man's questions of origins, though no-one explains what caused the big bang or how 'nothing' can somehow explode into something. People are happy not to ask too many questions. As a result, our modern world is very secular. Because of this, it has been felt by many that we no longer need God. For them there is no Creator, no God who rules and therefore no Judge. Man came from nowhere and is going nowhere. There is no binding moral law. There is little or no fear of God in society. Many people hold to a form of scientific materialism. Man has no soul and death is the end. Life expires like a candle that burns out. Similarly, they argue that we can therefore know nothing about the future of the world. It is up to chance. Perhaps the world will go on for millions of years, or maybe it will end in a nuclear holocaust, or, perhaps, pollution will make life on earth impossible. There are many today who fear that the world will end with man-made climate change. But the Bible teaches that God created the world and all true Christians believe this. He is also the God of providence who preserves and looks after the world. Further, He will one day bring the world to an end by the return of His Son and all will be judged and receive their eternal rewards according to their work.

Sadly, within the Christian church the growth of higher criticism and liberal theology have undermined belief in the afterlife. Liberal theologians like Rudolf Bultmann (1884-1976) say Jesus' resurrection was not physical but simply a rising in the faith of His disciples. He did not actually, materially, rise from the dead. Similarly, liberal teachers argue that when people die, they live on only in the memory of loved ones. Other ministers, who are not quite so extreme, are greatly influenced by the idea of the general fatherhood of God and the fact that the Bible says 'God is love' (1 John 4:8). They argue that all must eventually end up in Heaven whatever

INTRODUCTION

their works or whether they believed in Christ or not. Some talk of what is called 'conditional immortality'. They say the soul of man is not immortal and only true believers in Christ live forever. Generally speaking, within the Christian church today there is little preaching on Hell and the wrath to come. We, however, must not be influenced by the society around us or even by the church around us but rather follow the teaching of Scripture. It is the sure foundation and the 'only rule to direct us how we may glorify and enjoy God' (*Westminster Shorter Catechism*, Answer 2).

CHAPTER 1

OLD TESTAMENT TEACHING

The Fall
When God created man, He made him in His own image in knowledge, righteousness and holiness. Man was created with an immortal soul that will never die. The purpose of His creation was so that man would glorify and enjoy God. He was to have fellowship with his Maker. God entered into a covenant of life with him. Man was placed on probation. He was given a very beautiful place to live in, the garden of Eden, which contained all that he needed for a happy God-glorifying life. It was paradise and God Himself walked in the garden and fellowshipped with Adam and Eve. Eden was similar to the description of Heaven in Revelation 22 and contained the tree of life in the middle of the garden. However, there was one great difference from the future paradise. There was in the garden of Eden the 'Tree of knowledge of good and evil'. God's first covenant with man, the covenant of works, stated: 'But of the tree of the knowledge of good and evil, thou shalt not eat of it: for in the day that thou eatest thereof thou shalt surely die' (Genesis 2:17). Eternal life was promised to man if he did not eat the forbidden fruit, but death was decreed if he did eat the fruit.

Sadly, our first parents listened to the serpent, Satan, and broke God's covenant by eating the forbidden fruit. Immediately they felt naked and vulnerable before God. They had died spiritually. God came into the garden and pronounced His curse: 'Dust thou art, and unto dust shalt thou return' (Genesis 3:19). Physical death was coming to them. The ageing process began immediately and it would be followed by physical death, the separation of body and soul. They were expelled from the garden and from the presence of God. The first sin of man led to death spiritual (separation from God), death natural (separation of body and soul) and, without salvation, would lead to death eternal (eternal misery in Hell and separation from God forever).

Thankfully, at the same time, God revealed the gospel to our first parents. He told them about the provisions of the covenant of grace: 'And I will put enmity between thee and the woman, and between thy seed and her seed; it shall bruise thy head, and thou shalt bruise his heel' (Genesis 3:15). A child would be born to the woman who would crush the serpent's head and in the process His heel would be crushed. This was further illustrated by God providing them with a covering for their nakedness: 'Unto Adam also and to his wife did the Lord God make coats of skins, and clothed them' (v21). Animals were killed in order to be skinned to provide a covering for the nakedness of Adam and Eve before a holy God. These animals were types of the Christ who would die to provide an atonement for sinners. The Hebrew word for atonement is *kepher* or covering. Jesus died to provide us with a robe of righteousness to cover us, in the place of the useless rags, fig leaves, of our own self-righteousness. Christ is our hiding place.

Covenant with Noah

After the Fall the world deteriorated morally and spiritually very quickly. Cain, the first man born, murdered his godly brother Abel. Because of the immorality and violence of the ancient world, God destroyed it with a flood, that is with drastic and catastrophic climate change. Following the flood, however, God made a covenant with all mankind which contained a promise: 'I will not again curse the ground any more for man's sake; for the imagination of man's heart is evil from his youth; neither will I again smite any more every thing living, as I have done. While the earth remaineth, seedtime and harvest, and cold and heat, and summer and winter, and day and night shall not cease' (Genesis 8:21-22). God promised that the seasons would continue and that harvests would continue. God undertook to care for the world and man in it. Further God gave a rainbow as a sign of His covenant: 'This is the token of the covenant which I make between me and you and every living creature that is with you, for perpetual generations: I do set my bow in the cloud, and it shall be for a token of a covenant between me and the earth' (Genesis 9:12-13). Looking into the future the prophets of doom say that the world will become uninhabitable because of climate change. Modern man does not believe in God and therefore finds no comfort in Divine providence and the covenant made with Noah. Some young folk are very troubled almost to the point of despair with the continuing emission of greenhouse gases and what they call man-made climate change. But, despite man's unbelief, God's covenant ensures that 'seedtime and harvest' will not cease. God is preserving the world and man will not be able to destroy it.

Covenant with Abraham

God called Abraham out of idolatry in Ur of the Chaldees and made His covenant of grace with him. He promised: 'I will bless them that bless thee, and curse him that curseth thee: and in thee shall all families of the earth be blessed' (Genesis 12:3). God further promised Abraham: 'Look now toward heaven, and tell the stars, if thou be able to number them: and he said unto him, So shall thy seed be. And he believed in the Lord; and he counted it to him for righteousness' (Genesis 15:5-6). Abraham was made by God the father of the faithful. For centuries the people of God would be largely limited to the physical descendants of Abraham and Jacob, but the promise is that eventually all the families of the earth will be blessed. Salvation would come through the great Child of Abraham who is also the Seed of the woman earlier revealed to Adam and Eve: 'In thy seed shall all the nations of the earth be blessed' (Genesis 22:18). The church will grow to such an extent that it is not a mere remnant that will be saved but the church will be as numerous as the stars. Further, it is not just some families of the earth that will be blessed but so many will be blessed that it can legitimately be said that all the families of the earth will be blessed. Following the resurrection of Christ and the giving of the Spirit at Pentecost, the gospel is to be preached to all nations and the church of God will eventually be as the sand of the sea for multitude. The promised future of the church is exceedingly bright, so Christians are to have an optimistic eschatology.

Old Testament Saints and the Afterlife

Sometimes it is asserted that the saints in Old Testament times had no clear understanding of life after death and of Heaven and Hell. However, this can be clearly shown to be wrong. We are told, for example, of Enoch, that he walked with God: 'Enoch walked with God: and he was not; for God took him' (Genesis 5:24). It is obvious that he (body and soul) went to Heaven where the souls of other saints go when they die, as they await the resurrection of the last day. Jude tells us: 'Enoch also, the seventh from Adam, prophesied of these, saying, Behold, the Lord cometh with ten thousands of his saints, to execute judgment upon all, and to convince all that are ungodly among them of all their ungodly deeds which they have ungodly committed, and of all their hard speeches which ungodly sinners have spoken against him' (Jude 14-15). We are told that Enoch, in his own day, clearly declared the coming of the Lord and that there would be a judgment day for the wicked.

The Epistle to the Hebrews tells us concerning Abraham that he had the expectation of going to Heaven: 'By faith he sojourned in the land of promise, as in a strange country, dwelling in tabernacles with Isaac and Jacob, the heirs with him of the same promise: For he looked for a city which hath foundations, whose builder and maker is God' (Hebrews 11:9-10). Further it is written, 'But now they desire a better country, that is, an heavenly: wherefore God is not ashamed to be called their God: for he hath prepared for them a city' (v16). The land of promise was to Abraham a type of Heaven. By living in temporary tents the Patriarchs declared that this world was not their permanent home. They were looking for an eternal dwelling place.

Job displays his faith when in the midst of his horrendous trials he exclaims: 'I know that my Redeemer liveth, and that he shall stand at the latter day upon the earth: And though after my skin worms destroy this body, yet in my flesh shall I see God: whom I shall see for myself, and mine eyes shall behold, and not another' (Job 19:25-27). He shows here that he believes in a physical resurrection. His body will rot in the grave but one day will be raised again. He looks forward to seeing God and he believes that he will see God, 'in my flesh'.

There are many passages in the Psalms which show that the Old Testament saints believed in the afterlife. Psalm 16 is quoted by Peter in his Pentecostal sermon with reference to Christ, and while it specially and prophetically refers to Him it obviously also has a reference to all believers: 'My flesh also shall rest in hope. For thou wilt not leave my soul in hell; neither wilt thou suffer thine Holy One to see corruption. Thou wilt shew me the path of life: in thy presence is fulness of joy; at thy right hand there are pleasures for evermore' (Psalm 16:9-11). In the following Psalm there is another reference to the resurrection. After death the Psalmist will awake to see God: 'As for me, I will behold thy face in righteousness: I shall be satisfied, when I awake, with thy likeness' (Psalm 17:15). Psalm 23 is often sung at funerals: 'Surely goodness and mercy shall follow me all the days of my life: and I will dwell in the house of the Lord for ever' (v.6). Psalm 84 also clearly speaks of Heaven: 'They go from strength to strength, every one of them in Zion appeareth before God' (Psalm 84:7).

The coming judgment day is also clearly portrayed in the Psalms. The Psalmist speaks of the blessedness of the godly and then states: 'The ungodly are not so: but are like the chaff which the wind driveth away. Therefore the ungodly shall not stand in the judgment, nor sinners in the congregation of the righteous' (Psalm 1:4-5). Sinners are warned of their need to make peace with the Son of God, because there is a coming day of His wrath: 'Kiss the Son, lest he be angry, and ye perish from the way, when his wrath is kindled but a little. Blessed are all they that put their trust in him' (Psalm 2:12). The Psalmist in Psalm 73 is troubled when he sees the prosperity of the wicked in this life. They even seem to have an easy death, but then he visits the temple and realises their ultimate end: 'I went into the sanctuary of God; then understood I their end. Surely thou didst set them in slippery places: thou castedst them down into destruction' (Psalm 73:17-18).

Solomon describes death: 'Then shall the dust return to the earth as it was: and the spirit shall return unto God who gave it' (Ecclesiastes 12:7). The godly have a blessed future: 'The path of the just is as the shining light, that shineth more and more unto the perfect day' (Proverbs 4:18). The wicked are warned of the coming judgment: 'Rejoice, O young man, in thy youth; and let thy heart cheer thee in the days of thy youth, and walk in the ways of thine heart, and in the sight of thine eyes: but know thou, that for all these things God will bring thee into judgment' (Ecclesiastes 11:9).

The prophets also speak with assurance concerning the afterlife. Isaiah describes Heaven: 'Thy sun shall no more go down; neither shall thy moon withdraw itself: for the Lord shall be thine everlasting light, and the days of thy mourning shall be ended' (Isaiah 60:20). He also speaks of Hell, 'And they shall go forth, and look upon the carcases of the men that have transgressed against me: for their worm shall not die, neither shall their fire be quenched; and they shall be an abhorring unto all flesh' (Isaiah 66:24). Malachi writes of the future: 'For, behold, the day cometh, that shall burn as an oven; and all the proud, yea, and all that do wickedly, shall be stubble: and the day that cometh shall burn them up, saith the Lord of hosts, that it shall leave them neither root nor branch' (Malachi 4:1).

Surely no one reading the Old Testament can doubt that it speaks of the resurrection and judgment of the righteous and the wicked when they consider the prophecy of Daniel: 'And many of them that sleep in the dust of the earth shall awake, some to everlasting life, and some to shame and everlasting contempt. And they that be wise shall shine as the brightness of the firmament; and they that turn many to righteousness as the stars for ever and ever' (Daniel 12:2-3)!

Prophecies of the Coming of Christ

Throughout the Old Testament there is a promise of the coming Messiah and a longing for Him to come. We are first told of His coming in the curse on the serpent which is the so-called *proto-evangelium*, or first statement of the gospel: 'And I will put enmity between thee and the woman, and between thy seed and her seed; it shall bruise thy head, and thou shalt bruise his heel' (Genesis 3:15). Abel looked forward in faith to the dying Saviour who would sacrifice Himself for him: 'By faith Abel offered unto God a more excellent sacrifice than Cain, by which he obtained witness that he was righteous, God testifying of his gifts: and by it he being dead yet speaketh' (Hebrews 11:4). Abraham looked for the coming Seed, because Jesus said: 'Your father Abraham rejoiced to see my day: and he saw it, and was glad' (John 8:56). Moses spoke by divine revelation of the great Messianic Prophet: 'I will raise them up a Prophet from among their brethren, like unto thee, and will put my words in his mouth; and he shall speak unto them all that I shall command him. And it shall come to pass, that whosoever will not hearken unto my words which he shall speak in my name, I will require it of him' (Deuteronomy 18:18-19). David prophesied of the coming Priest and King: 'The Lord hath sworn, and will not repent, Thou art a priest for ever after the order of Melchizedek. The Lord at thy right hand shall strike through kings in the day of his wrath. He shall judge among the heathen' (Psalm 110:4-6). Concerning the coming One, Isaiah foretells: 'For unto us a child is born, unto us a son is given: and the government shall be upon his shoulder: and his name shall be called Wonderful, Counsellor, The mighty God, The everlasting Father, The Prince of Peace. Of the increase of his government and peace there shall be no end, upon the throne of David, and upon his kingdom, to order it, and to establish it with judgment and with justice from henceforth even for ever' (Isaiah 9:6-7).

So we see that the faithful in Old Testament times looked forward to this mighty Saviour who was to come, the greatest Prophet, Priest and King. He is none other than the Lord. He will reign for ever. But He would also suffer as the suffering Servant of the Lord. Indeed, this coming Priest would offer Himself as a sacrifice for the sins of His people: 'But he was wounded for our transgressions, he was bruised for our iniquities: the chastisement of our peace was upon him; and with his stripes we are healed. All we like sheep have gone astray; we have turned every one to his own way; and the Lord hath laid on him the iniquity of us all' (Isaiah 53:5-6). The prophet then adds: 'Yet it pleased the Lord to bruise him; he hath put him to grief: when thou shalt make his soul an offering for sin, he shall see his seed, he shall prolong his days, and the pleasure of the Lord shall prosper in his hand' (Isaiah 53:10). He will suffer and die for the sins of His people but with these very words there is reference also to His triumphant resurrection, 'He shall see his seed, he shall prolong his days, and the pleasure of the Lord shall prosper in his hand'. Though cut off He shall prolong His days. We today are saved by looking back to Calvary and putting our faith in the One who suffered there for our sins. In Old Testament times they were also saved by faith, but their faith looked forward to the coming Messiah and His suffering in their room and place.

Prophetic Perspective

One problem that we have in many of the Old Testament prophecies of the coming Messiah is that the first and second comings of Christ seem to be combined. Think for example of Malachi's prophecy: 'Behold, I will send my messenger, and he shall prepare the way before me: and the Lord, whom ye seek, shall suddenly come to his temple, even the messenger of the covenant, whom ye delight in: behold, he shall come, saith the Lord of hosts. But who may abide the day of his coming? and who shall stand when he appeareth? for he is like a refiner's fire, and like fullers' soap: And he shall sit as a refiner and purifier of silver: and he shall purify the sons of Levi, and purge them as gold and silver, that they may offer unto the Lord an offering in righteousness' (Malachi 3:1-3). The messenger preparing the way is obviously a reference to John the Baptist. This is confirmed by Matthew 3:3 in describing the ministry of John. The Messenger of the covenant is the Lord for whom John prepared the way. He will come suddenly and unexpected by most. But then we read of Him judging men and women. Yet Jesus said, 'I came not to judge the world, but to save the world' (John 12:47). There is here an obvious reference also to His second coming. The two comings of Christ are merged into one. This is best explained when the future is considered from the perspective of the Old Testament prophet. It is rather like a traveller seeing a mountain range in the distance. All the mountains appear to be one range but when the traveller gets closer he can see that there are actually two mountain ranges one in front of the other and, perhaps, many miles between the two. In a similar way the two comings of the Messiah are seen together though they are thousands of years apart.

Joel prophesies concerning the coming of the day of the Lord: 'And it shall come to pass afterward, that I will pour out my spirit upon all flesh; and your sons and your daughters shall prophesy, your old men shall dream dreams, your young men shall see visions: And also upon the servants and upon the handmaids in those days will I pour out my spirit. And I will shew wonders in the heavens and in the earth, blood, and fire, and pillars of smoke. The sun shall be turned into darkness, and the moon into blood, before the great and terrible day of the Lord come. And it shall come to pass, that whosoever shall call on the name of the Lord shall be delivered: for in mount Zion and in Jerusalem shall be deliverance, as the Lord hath said, and in the remnant whom the Lord shall call' (Joel 2:28-32). Peter assures us that this was fulfilled on the day of Pentecost: 'But this is that which was spoken by the prophet Joel; And it shall come to pass in the last days, saith God, I will pour out of my Spirit upon all flesh: and your sons and your daughters shall prophesy, and your young men shall see visions, and your old men shall dream dreams' (Acts 2:16-17). The pouring out of God's Holy Spirit was an amazing and wonderful redemptive-historical event. But in the words of Joel there is much that obviously refers to the second coming of Christ: 'The sun shall be turned into darkness, and the moon into blood, before the great and terrible day of the Lord come'. This must refer to the end of the world, the second coming of Christ and the great judgment day. From the perspective of the Old Testament prophet both comings of Christ merge into one.

It will be important in the following chapters as we consider New Testament prophecies of the future that we remember this principle of interpretation gleaned from the Old Testament prophecies concerning the viewing of the first and second comings of our Lord as if they were merged into one. This will be especially relevant when considering for example Matthew 24 where Christ's prophecies of the destruction of

OLD TESTAMENT TEACHING

Jerusalem and of the end of the world are described.

CHAPTER 2

DEATH

The Reality of Death

Death is a huge reality that faces every one of us. All around us we see people dying, grandparents, parents, siblings and sometimes even our own children. Scripture says, 'It is appointed unto men once to die, but after this the judgment' (Hebrews 9:27). Nothing seems more natural than death. Benjamin Franklin wrote in a letter to Jean-Baptiste Le Roy in 1789 with reference to the American Constitution: 'Our new Constitution is now established, and has an appearance that promises permanency; but in this world nothing can be said to be certain, except death and taxes'. It may indeed be possible to avoid taxes but there is no escape from death. Every living creature around us is dying. Each one of us from the moment we are born is terminally ill and slowly dying.

The Origin of Death

However, death is not natural. It was not there in the beginning. When God created the world in the beginning it was full of life and there was no death anywhere. Adam was created in the image of God, for fellowship with God. God entered into a covenant with him, promising him life on condition of perfect obedience, but threatening death on disobedience. If he obeyed God he would live forever. But there was in the middle of the garden of Eden the tree of knowledge of good and evil. God in His covenant said to Adam, 'Of every tree of the garden thou mayest freely eat: but of the tree of the knowledge of good and evil, thou shalt not eat of it: for in the day that thou eatest thereof thou shalt surely die' (Genesis 2:16-17). Sadly, our first parents ate the forbidden fruit and so fell from the state in which they were created into a state of sin and misery. So the world became a place where death reigned instead of being, as it originally was, full of life.

Sometimes the point is made that Adam did not die in the day on which he ate the fruit. He actually lived on for another nine hundred and thirty years. But to argue in this way fails to take account of what really happened. There are three kinds of death spoken of in Scripture. First, there is natural death which is the separation of body and soul. That began as a process of ageing immediately Adam ate the fruit. Then there is spiritual death. This is spiritual separation from God. This took place immediately. It was evidenced in that Adam felt naked and ashamed. When God came into the garden he and Eve ran away to hide. The loving relationship in which he was created had changed. Man was now under God's wrath and curse. Then, thirdly, there is eternal death. This is what happens when an unconverted sinner dies and is sent forever to Hell. It is an existence eternally separated from God and all His blessings. But it is not simply missing what is good. It is also being forever tormented by the just wrath of God. When Adam sinned he and Eve died spiritually to God and natural death began to work in their bodies. Thankfully, the sentence of eternal death was not carried out immediately. God in his great long-suffering gave Adam time, and in His mercy proclaimed the gospel to Adam telling him of the coming Saviour (Genesis 3:15). God allowed man to continue to live in this world, giving to him a day of grace in which he could repent and be converted and so escape from eternal death. Because we were represented by Adam our covenant head in the garden of Eden, we sinned in him and fell with him in his first transgression. We also ate the forbidden fruit and so are sinners before we are born, even before we are conceived, and so, too, every one of us is born dead, spiritually dead.

Imputation

The truth of imputation is wonderfully presented by Paul in Romans: 'For as by one man's disobedience many were made sinners, so by the obedience of one shall many be made righteous' (Romans 5:19). God, when He created Adam, appointed him to be the covenant head and representative of the human race. The Apostle here is arguing that, because of this, when Adam disobeyed God, we too disobeyed. We were represented in him so that when he sinned, we sinned. In the same way the elect are represented in Christ. Christ's perfect obedience to His Father, keeping the law in every detail, as well as His suffering the punishment for sin, becomes ours if we are in Christ in the covenant of grace. By the obedience of one, many were made righteous. Paul states: 'Death reigned from Adam to Moses, even over them that had not sinned after the similitude of Adam's transgression, who is the figure of him that was to come. But not as the offence, so also is the free gift. For if through the offence of one many be dead, much more the grace of God, and the gift by grace, which is by one man, Jesus Christ, hath abounded unto many. And not as it was by one that sinned, so is the gift: for the judgment was by one to condemnation, but the free gift is of many offences unto justification. For if by one man's offence death reigned by one; much more they which receive abundance of grace and of the gift of righteousness shall reign in life by one, Jesus Christ. Therefore as by the offence of one judgment came upon all men to condemnation; even so by the righteousness of one the free gift came upon all men unto justification of life' (Romans 5:14-18). In the original covenant the first Adam's sin was ours and brought about our condemnation. However, in a similar way, wonderfully, the last Adam's obedience, Christ's obedience, is ours and makes us righteous. One sin condemned us but Christ's work obtains pardon for those guilty of many offences. This salvation is available to all as a free gift. The only requirement of the covenant of grace is to receive Christ by faith. So faith in the finished work of Christ is the condition for imputation and justification.

Later in the same epistle, Paul writes: 'For the wages of sin is death; but the gift of God is eternal life through Jesus Christ our Lord' (Romans 5:21). Every sin is rebellion against God and demands a response from God. It is a work for which payment is made. Unlike some human employers, God always pays wages in full. Our sinful works earn wages which are either paid to us or were paid to Christ in our place. The one condition of the covenant of grace is faith. Those who believe in the Lord

DEATH

Jesus Christ benefit from Christ taking the wages for their sins. 'Being justified by faith, we have peace with God through our Lord Jesus Christ' (Romans 5:1). Christ is freely offered to all to be their Saviour and all who receive Him have their sins forgiven. When we believe in Jesus all our sins, past, present and future are forgiven.

Long lives

It is interesting to notice at this stage that the early inhabitants of the world lived much longer than we do today, despite the advances in modern medicine and surgery. Methuselah lived for nine hundred and sixty-nine years. How was this? Perhaps, as some have suggested, before the great deposits of coal and oil were formed at the time of the flood, greenhouse gases such as carbon dioxide covered the earth and protected the inhabitants from harmful cosmic and ultraviolet rays. Perhaps too the various harmful diseases and viruses which are common in our world today took time to develop. The flood certainly brought about catastrophic climate change. The flood itself came because the wickedness and violence of man had grown to intolerable levels. God decided, 'My spirit shall not always strive with man, for that he also is flesh: yet his days shall be an hundred and twenty years' (Genesis 6:3). Now the 120 years here, no doubt refers first and foremost to the remaining time before the world would be destroyed by the flood and therefore the time that Noah was given in which to build the ark, but it would seem also that from now on 120 years would normally be the maximum length of man's life. We are told that, 'God saw that the wickedness of man was great in the earth, and that every imagination of the thoughts of his heart was only evil continually. And it repented the Lord that he had made man on the earth, and it grieved him at his heart' (Genesis 6:5-6). God hates sin and in His common grace limits it. He notes that the 'imagination of man's heart is evil from his youth' (Genesis 8:21). God's long-suffering is great in allowing a life of threescore and ten (Psalm 90:10), or occasionally 120 years like Moses, but God has decided that that is a long enough time for man on earth to allow him to repent and be converted.

THE GLORIOUS FUTURE

All creation affected

The sin of man did not just affect the human race. Man was the crown of creation and therefore his sin brought a curse upon the whole world. The animal kingdom was affected in many ways. God said to the serpent: 'Because thou hast done this, thou art cursed above all cattle, and above every beast of the field; upon thy belly shalt thou go, and dust shalt thou eat all the days of thy life' (Genesis 3:14). The implication is that, instead of walking, snakes would now have to slither. With reference to the plant world it is said, 'Thorns also and thistles shall it bring forth to thee; and thou shalt eat the herb of the field' (Genesis 3:18). Weeds would now grow more readily than useful plants and man would have to sweat to feed his family. Pain comes to the woman even in childbirth. What a wonderful blessing it is to have a child but all good things in this life have their negative side because of sin! The whole of creation and life in general is under God's curse and suffers pain. Death is universal and that which leads to death – sickness and suffering – comes to every living creature.

Paul picks up this theme when he states: 'For the creature was made subject to vanity, not willingly, but by reason of him who hath subjected the same in hope, Because the creature itself also shall be delivered from the bondage of corruption into the glorious liberty of the children of God. For we know that the whole creation groaneth and travaileth in pain together until now. And not only they, but ourselves also, which have the firstfruits of the Spirit, even we ourselves groan within ourselves, waiting for the adoption, to wit, the redemption of our body' (Romans 8:20-23). Wherever we look in the world there is pain and suffering. Nature is red in tooth and claw. In the animal kingdom, among the birds and the fish, there is fighting, killing and eating one another. Even the inanimate creation groans. There are storms, earthquakes, volcanoes, tsunamis, typhoons, and hurricanes all demonstrating a world writhing in pain looking forward to the regeneration, the birth of the new heavens and new earth when the children of God will be revealed and Christ's returning will usher in His eternal kingdom.

DEATH

Death

The words of our Saviour on the cross are very interesting and important: 'And when Jesus had cried with a loud voice, he said, Father, into thy hands I commend my spirit: and having said thus, he gave up the ghost' (Luke 23:46). He voluntarily dismissed His spirit. He did not die in weakness as you and I will die. Just before He died, He cried with a loud voice to show His continuing strength. He had earlier said of His life, 'No man taketh it from me, but I lay it down of myself. I have power to lay it down, and I have power to take it again. This commandment have I received of my Father' (John 10:18). Death had no claim upon Him because He was sinless but He willingly offered Himself as a sin offering for us and gave Himself to death.

When the time comes for us to die we have no choice. People talk of fighting cancer and imply that they can resist death, but death always wins. God has appointed the day of our birth and the day of our death. When God calls us to give our account to Him none can say 'No!' As Solomon wrote, 'Then shall the dust return to the earth as it was: and the spirit shall return unto God who gave it' (Ecclesiastes 12:7). However, there is all the difference in the world between the death of the Christian and the death of the unbeliever. For the Christian, death is the doorway to glory but for the unbeliever, death involves the sentence of condemnation. Death for the child of God is an exciting new beginning. In contrast, the Psalmist says of the death of the wicked: 'Surely thou didst set them in slippery places: thou castedst them down into destruction. How are they brought into desolation, as in a moment! They are utterly consumed with terrors' (Psalm 73:18-19).

Stephen was the first Christian martyr following the resurrection of Christ. To prepare him for death he was given a vision of Heaven. He could see the Lord Jesus standing up to receive him. He was so filled with the Spirit of God that his face shone like an angel. We are told that, 'they stoned Stephen, calling upon God, and saying, Lord Jesus, receive my spirit. And he kneeled down, and cried with a loud voice, Lord, lay not this sin to their charge. And when he had said this, he fell asleep' (Acts 7:59-60). What a glorious and victorious death that was!

Falling asleep

It is interesting to notice the difference that the New Testament makes between the death of the Christian and the death of the unconverted. The Christian's death is always called falling asleep, but that term is never used for the death of the wicked. Falling asleep is such a lovely picture. There is nothing more peaceful. It is true that death is called the Christian's last enemy (1 Corinthians 15:26), but it is the *last* enemy and once death comes there are no more enemies. The body is buried and rests in the grave till the resurrection, but the soul is immediately transported to Heaven. The Thessalonians felt sad that some of their number died before the second coming of Christ. Paul assures them that those who have died will not miss out: 'But I would not have you to be ignorant, brethren, concerning them which are asleep, that ye sorrow not, even as others which have no hope. For if we believe that Jesus died and rose again, even so them also which sleep in Jesus will God bring with him' (1 Thessalonians 4:13-14). Those who die before Christ returns will be with Jesus in Heaven and will return with Him at the end of the world.

What the Catechism teaches

The *Westminster Shorter Catechism* gives a very helpful and informative answer to the question (Q37):

> 'What benefits do believers receive from Christ at death?'

Answer:
> 'The souls of believers are, at their death, made perfect in holiness, and do immediately pass into glory; and their bodies, being still united to Christ, do rest in their graves till the resurrection'.

The process of sanctification begins the moment we are born again and continues throughout this life, but it is not completed while we are still here in this life. No one reaches a state of perfection in this world. John makes that very clear: 'If we say that we have no sin, we deceive ourselves, and the truth is not in us ... If we say that we have not sinned, we make him a liar, and his word is not in us' (1 John 1:8, 10). However, the moment we die, sanctification is perfected. The process is completed. We are made fit for Heaven and the Scripture speaks of 'the spirits of just men made perfect' (Hebrews 12:23). All who are justified will be made perfect in their souls when they die.

The *Catechism* states that the bodies of Christians are still united to Christ while they are dead in the grave. This is amazing. How could a rotting body be united to God? The reason for this is that when we become Christians we are united to Christ. The Spirit of Christ indwells us and takes possession of us. Our bodies become temples of the Holy Spirit and God dwells in us. Another way of looking at this change is that we are brought into Christ at conversion and we become part of His body. Christ is the head and Christians are the members of the body (1 Corinthians 12). Now human beings are not just souls. We are composed of both bodies and souls: 'And the Lord God formed man of the dust of the ground, and breathed into his nostrils the breath of life; and man became a living soul' (Genesis 2:7). When we are converted our body and soul, that is our whole person, is united to Christ. That union is eternal and can never be broken. Paul states: 'For I am persuaded, that neither death, nor life ... shall be able to separate us from the love of God, which is in Christ Jesus our Lord' (Romans 8:38-39). Thus, our bodies are precious and are to be treated with great respect. Whatever happens to our bodies they are united to Christ and then at the resurrection they are raised from the dead.

Soul Sleep

One of the heresies that has been around for a long time and is still here today is the idea that when we die the soul sleeps or goes into some kind of suspended state. Eusebius, in the early church, refers to a small sect in Arabia who adhered to this position and then there were also some Anabaptists at the Reformation, and later, in the nineteenth century, the Irvingites who held this view. The Jehovah's Witnesses teach this today. Various arguments are raised in its support. For example, the term sleep is used for death, but it should be remembered that it is the body which sleeps and not the soul. It is sometimes argued that when individuals are raised from the dead they say nothing about the state they had been in before being raised. But this could simply be explained by their memories being blanked by God. Alternatively, it could be that they were not allowed to say what they saw and experienced. Paul once had an amazing vision into Heaven: 'I knew such a man, (whether in the body, or out of the body, I cannot tell: God knoweth;) how that he was caught up into paradise, and heard unspeakable words, which it is not lawful for a man to utter' (2 Corinthians 12:3-4). The vision was so real to him that he was not sure if he had been bodily transported into Heaven or simply in his mind. He adds that he heard words 'which it is not lawful for a man to utter'. He was not allowed to say what he had heard. That may be the case also with those raised from the dead.

Another argument is that the traditional view would require two judgment days, one when the individual dies and another at the end of the world. We accept that. Immediately a person dies they are sent either to Heaven or Hell. However, this argument about the two judgment days fails to understand the purpose of the final judgment day. It is not for settling the final state of an individual but for vindicating God's justice and publicly displaying the wickedness of the wicked and the good works of the righteous. It is for openly acknowledging and acquitting the people of God.

There are various passages of Scripture that clearly teach the consciousness of the soul after death. For example, Jesus says to the thief on the cross, 'Today shalt thou be with me in paradise' (Luke 23:43). The converted thief was not heading for some dreamy, grey place of sleep but for the joys of paradise. Paul speaks of the tension he felt, on the one hand desiring to die and be in a blessed Heaven, and on the other hand wishing to remain so that he could benefit the church: 'For to me to live is Christ, and to die is gain. But if I live in the flesh, this is the fruit of my labour: yet what I shall choose I wot not. For I am in a strait betwixt two, having a desire to depart, and to be with Christ; which is far better: Nevertheless to abide in the flesh is more needful for you' (Philippians 1:21-24). It is far better to die because of the blessings of paradise which he will enjoy in his soul. At the end of his life he looks forward to dying because he knows the bliss awaiting him: 'For I am now ready to be offered, and the time of my departure is at hand. I have fought a good fight, I have finished my course, I have kept the faith: Henceforth there is laid up for me a crown of righteousness, which the Lord, the righteous judge, shall give me at that day: and not to me only, but unto all them also that love his appearing' (2 Timothy 4:6-8).

Purgatory

Roman Catholic theology teaches that there are three states beyond death. The unbaptised wicked go straight to Hell. The saints, a very small number of mankind who have earned God's favour by their good works, go straight to Heaven. Most Christians, they say, go to Purgatory for further purification before they can enter Heaven. There they will be subjected to fire and torment because of their sins. Prayers and masses can be offered for the dead so that their stay in Purgatory will be shortened. The church on earth has the power to grant indulgences so that the time spent in Purgatory is reduced.

But the Scriptures make plain that when death comes we enter our final state: 'If the tree fall toward the south, or toward the north, in the place where the tree falleth, there it shall be' (Ecclesiastes 11:3). This doctrine of Purgatory has no support in the Scriptures but very much the contrary. It denies the sufficiency of the work of Christ in making full atonement for all our sins. It is therefore an attack upon the work of Christ. It undermines the Bible's teaching of justification by faith alone. The Lord Jesus bore all our sins and was punished fully in our place. 'There is therefore now no condemnation to them which are in Christ Jesus' (Romans 8:1). Our sufferings anyway could never atone for our sins. 'But he was wounded for our transgressions, he was bruised for our iniquities: the chastisement of our peace was upon him; and with his stripes we are healed' (Isaiah 53:5). Yes, in this life, we are chastised and corrected and the fires of trial purify us, but the Christian is never punished. Christ endured all punishment in our place: 'Therefore being justified by faith, we have peace with God through our Lord Jesus Christ' (Romans 5:1). In fact Christ purged our sins before He ascended up to Heaven, 'when he had by himself purged our sins, sat down on the right hand of the Majesty on high' (Hebrews 1:3). All the sins of the elect were atoned for and divine justice satisfied 2000 years ago at Calvary. There are only the two places in the next world, the glories and joys of Heaven and the misery of Hell.

Rich man and Lazarus
The parable of the rich man and Lazarus is very helpful in teaching what happens at death (Luke 16:19-31). We note that there is no purgatory here, only Heaven and Hell. An obvious contrast is drawn between the rich man and the beggar in their lives in this world: 'There was a certain rich man, which was clothed in purple and fine linen, and fared sumptuously every day: And there was a certain beggar named Lazarus, which was laid at his gate, full of sores, And desiring to be fed with the crumbs which fell from the rich man's table: moreover the dogs came and licked his sores' (Luke 16:19-21). One appeared to have all the good things and the other all the miseries but the beggar's name Lazarus is significant. 'Lazarus' is the Greek equivalent of the Hebrew 'Eliezer'. It means, 'his help is in God'. A further contrast is noticed in their death. Lazarus has angels around him as he dies and they carry his soul to Heaven. The rich man presumably has devils around his bedside and they carry his soul to Hell: 'the rich man also died, and was buried; And in hell he lift up his eyes, being in torments' (vv22-23). The nameless rich man is surrounded by every earthly comfort and medical aid, and no doubt given a huge funeral, but meanwhile he was in torments. The rich man asks that Lazarus be sent with a drop of water to comfort him in the flames. When that is refused he asks that Lazarus be sent to warn his brothers lest they end up in the same place. So obviously he was conscious in his misery immediately after death as was Lazarus of his joys in Heaven. The rich man was also suffering while his brothers enjoyed the pleasures of this world. From this it is plain that the soul does not sleep but goes immediately either to Heaven or Hell. It should be noted

that Lazarus did not go to heaven because he was poor, or because suffered in this life, but rather because he trusted in God. The name he is given indicated his faith.

The Intermediate State

A further fascinating passage of Scripture which deals with the state of the believer between death and the resurrection is 2 Corinthians 5. Here Paul states that the ultimate bliss follows the final resurrection: 'For we know that if our earthly house of this tabernacle were dissolved, we have a building of God, an house not made with hands, eternal in the heavens' (2 Corinthians 5:1). The earthly house which he refers to here is obviously the body in this world. One day soon each one of us will experience this body being dissolved. Soul and body will be parted. The lifeless body will be laid in the grave where it will decay. However, the dead will continue in conscious existence in their souls. Houses in this world are made by human hands but our eternal house or body will not be made by human hands but by God's hands. The eternal house is the resurrection body which will be fit for eternal existence. Paul says, 'For in this we groan, earnestly desiring to be clothed upon with our house which is from heaven: If so be that being clothed we shall not be found naked. For we that are in this tabernacle do groan, being burdened: not for that we would be unclothed, but clothed upon, that mortality might be swallowed up of life' (vv2-4). He states that we groan. We are longing for something that we do not have. We do not wish to be naked spirits. We do not wish to be unclothed but clothed upon. Our redemption is complete only following the resurrection.

Death and the separation of body and soul are the result of sin. It comes as the curse upon us as covenant breakers. But then at the resurrection all the effects of sin and the curse will be removed. Body and soul are united again. Mortality is swallowed up of life. Paul is asserting that the intermediate state where the soul is naked without its body is not ideal. Yet he asserts that it is still better than the present state, for 'whilst we are at home in the body, we are absent from the Lord' (v6). Being present here below in our bodies means that we are absent from the Lord.

Then he adds, 'We are confident, I say, and willing rather to be absent from the body, and to be present with the Lord' (v8). It is better to be absent from the body and present with the Lord. We have great comfort when our loved ones fall asleep in Jesus. We know that they are with Christ and therefore happy in Heaven. 'Blessed are the dead which die in the Lord from henceforth: Yea, saith the Spirit, that they may rest from their labours; and their works do follow them' (Revelation 14:13).

CHAPTER 3

EVENTS PRECEDING THE SECOND COMING

Having begun consideration of individual eschatology and dealt with death and the intermediate estate we should now turn to general eschatology and look at the events which lead to the Second Coming of Christ. The return of Christ is the great hope and expectation of the church.

Terms used for the Second Coming

Three terms are used in Scripture for the second coming of Christ.

(1) The first of these is *apokalupsis* which means revelation. It has the idea of the removal of the veil, showing something which is otherwise hidden. It is the term used by Paul when he says to the Corinthians, 'So that ye come behind in no gift; waiting for the *coming* of our Lord Jesus Christ: who shall also confirm you unto the end, that ye may be blameless in the day of our Lord Jesus Christ' (1 Corinthians 1:7-8). It is also used in 2 Thessalonians 1:6-7: 'Seeing it is a righteous thing with God to recompense tribulation to them that trouble you; and to you who are troubled rest with us, when the Lord Jesus shall be *revealed* from heaven with his mighty angels'.

(2) The second term is *epiphaneia* which means appearance, from which we get our term epiphany. Paul uses this term when he admonishes Timothy: 'That thou keep this commandment without spot, unrebukable, until the *appearing* of our Lord Jesus Christ' (1 Timothy 6:14).

(3) The third word used is *parousia* which means coming and is used for example in Matthew 24:27: 'For as the lightning cometh out of the east, and shineth even unto the west; so shall also the *coming* of the Son of man be'.

THE GLORIOUS FUTURE

The Promised Return
Our Lord Jesus told His disciples that He was going to have to leave them. This made them sad, but He assures them, 'I will not leave you comfortless' (John 14:18). He would not leave them like orphans. Indeed, He explained to them it would be for their benefit: 'Nevertheless I tell you the truth; It is expedient for you that I go away: for if I go not away, the Comforter will not come unto you; but if I depart, I will send him unto you' (John 16:7). The Comforter, the Holy Spirit, would be the abiding presence of Christ with the church and He would apply the redemption purchased by Christ to them. He would regenerate them, indwell them, sanctify them, assure them, guide them, empower them and glorify them. The Spirit would unite them to God. Jesus as a man was limited to being in one place at one time but the Spirit as God is omnipresent and able to help every Christian, wherever they are, and at the same time. Jesus further encourages His disciples: 'Let not your heart be troubled: ye believe in God, believe also in me. In my Father's house are many mansions: if it were not so, I would have told you. I go to prepare a place for you. And if I go and prepare a place for you, I will come again, and receive you unto myself; that where I am, there ye may be also' (John 14:1-3). He assures them that He will return again. On an earlier occasion He had warned them to be ready for His return: 'Watch therefore: for ye know not what hour your Lord doth come' (Matthew 24:42). When tried before Caiaphas He asserted: 'Hereafter shall ye see the Son of man sitting on the right hand of power, and coming in the clouds of heaven' (Matthew 26:64), and this caused the High Priest to rend his garments and condemn Jesus as a blasphemer, but our Saviour is the only man who never blasphemed. He spoke the truth. He will come again riding on the clouds of Heaven on the last day. Following His ascension, while the disciples were still gazing up into the skies into which their Lord disappeared, two angels stood by them in white clothes and said, 'Ye men of Galilee, why stand ye gazing up into heaven? this same Jesus, which is taken up from you into heaven, shall so come in like manner as ye have seen him go into heaven' (Acts 1:11). Christ will return one day visibly and bodily just as He ascended.

EVENTS PRECEDING THE SECOND COMING

When will Christ come again?

Down through the centuries people have tried to predict when Christ would return. The Jehovah's Witnesses first predicted that Christ's second coming would be in 1878. When it did not happen they predicted it would be in 1881. When that didn't happen they said it would be in 1914, then 1918, then 1925, then 1975. They are obviously false prophets. Much publicity some years ago was given to Harold Camping, president of Family Radio and a well-known Bible teacher who predicted that Christ would return in September 1994. He too was proved false.

In relation to His coming again, the Lord Jesus made an interesting confession when He said, 'But of that day and hour knoweth no man, no, not the angels of heaven, but my Father only' (Matthew 24:36). He is even more specific when He said: 'But of that day and that hour knoweth no man, no, not the angels which are in heaven, neither the Son, but the Father' (Mark 13:32). If it could be worked out from the Scriptures Jesus would have done that. He knew many things that we do not. He is the Word of God and the greatest Prophet there ever was, yet He tells us clearly that He, the Son, did not know the date of the second coming. As God, the Second Person, of course He is omniscient and knows everything but as a human being He is limited. He knows only what God through the Spirit chooses to reveal to Him. God had a purpose in keeping that date from Him at that time, and also from us. Our duty is made plain: 'Watch therefore, for ye know neither the day nor the hour wherein the Son of man cometh' (Matthew 25:13). We live in dangerous times. There are many false prophets around. In Old Testament times, someone who prophesied of a future event and it did not happen, was to be put to death (Deuteronomy 18:20-22). Under the civil law of the time, it was to be regarded as a serious crime of deception to claim to be speaking for God and to tell lies. Jesus also warned against those false prophets, 'Then if any man shall say unto you, Lo, here is Christ, or there; believe it not. For there shall arise false Christs, and false prophets, and shall shew great signs and wonders; insomuch that, if it were possible, they shall deceive the very elect' (Matthew 24:23-24). Yes, if it was possible even the elect would be deceived but that is not possible: 'But ye have an unction from the Holy One, and ye know all things' (1 John 2:20). Peter assures believers of their preservation, for they are those, 'Who are kept by the power of God through faith unto salvation ready to be revealed in the last time' (1 Peter 1:5).

Was Christ mistaken as to His return?
Liberal theologians think Christ was mistaken as to the time of His return. They say that He thought He would return in the lifetime of His disciples. In Matthew 24 we are told of many great things which were to happen, including His own return. Then Jesus says: 'Verily I say unto you, This generation shall not pass, till all these things be fulfilled. Heaven and earth shall pass away, but my words shall not pass away' (vv34-35). On the surface this seems to imply that His return would take place during the lifetime of some of those who were present. However, we totally reject liberal theology and its unbelief in suggesting that Christ was wrong about His return. If Jesus made mistakes, He is not the Son of God and He cannot save us. If His prediction of certain events was wrong, we cannot trust Him in anything He said. As real Christians therefore our starting point is the infallibility of Christ and of the Scriptures.

But how then are we to understand Jesus' teaching in Matthew 24? Some evangelicals follow what is called a Preterist understanding of this chapter. For them all that is prophesied in Matthew 24 and Mark 13, and also in Luke 21, has actually happened already. They see these events as fulfilled in the destruction of Jerusalem and the scattering of the Jewish nation in AD70. Jesus, they say, is using common apocalyptic language which to us seems very graphic to describe these dramatic events. They say we should not take this language literally. It is certainly possible to interpret these chapters in that way. However, to me this chapter goes well beyond the events of AD70 even allowing for the use here of apocalyptic language.

Others interpret it in a partly Preterist way. (A preterist is one who holds that the prophecies in the Bible about the End Times have already been fulfilled). They divide chapter 24 at the end of verse 35. What happened before verse 36 was fulfilled in the destruction of Jerusalem but then verses 36 on to the end of the chapter describe the end of the world. The language, however, even in the part before verse 36 does seem to go beyond what happened in the destruction of Jerusalem, dramatic though that event was. Surely what we read in verses 30-31 describes the second coming: 'And then shall appear the sign of the Son of man in heaven: and then shall all the tribes of the earth mourn, and they shall see the Son of man coming in the clouds of heaven with power and great glory. And he shall send his angels with a great sound of a trumpet, and they shall gather together his elect from the four winds, from one end of heaven to the other' (Matthew 24:30-31). Surely this can only refer to the end of the world and the final judgment.

Others argue that 'this generation shall not pass' refers to an evil and adulterous generation like the one then present. This type of generation will not pass till all is fulfilled and this type of generation is still with us today. Or alternatively that the Jewish race will not pass till all these things be fulfilled. But surely if this was the case the word used would be *'genos'*, kind, or race, rather than *'gennea'*, which means generation. In all the other cases in the New Testament when 'this generation' is used it refers to that actual generation, e.g., 'But whereunto shall I liken this generation? It is like unto children sitting in the markets, and calling unto their fellows' (Matthew 11:16). Our Lord here is clearly referring to the people alive at that time. Another example would be, 'The queen of the south shall rise up in the judgment with this generation, and shall condemn it: for she came from the uttermost parts of the earth to hear the wisdom of Solomon; and, behold, a greater than Solomon is here' (Matthew 12:42). Here also Jesus is talking about those who were actually alive in His day on earth and hearing Him.

A sound explanation of Matthew 24
The best way to understand what Jesus is saying here is to go back to the original questions He was asked. The chapter begins with the disciples showing our Lord the temple. They are obviously proud of the beautiful

buildings. Jesus responds to them, 'See ye not all these things? verily I say unto you, There shall not be left here one stone upon another, that shall not be thrown down' (Matthew 24:2). That must have shocked the disciples. It left questions in their mind. Later, as He sat resting on the mount of Olives, looking towards Jerusalem, the disciples came unto Him privately, asking, 'Tell us, when shall these things be? and what shall be the sign of thy coming, and of the end of the world?' (Matthew 24:3).

It is important, therefore, to notice that Jesus is here asked two different questions. First, He is asked when will the temple be destroyed? Then they ask a second question, What shall be the sign indicating His second coming and the end of the world? It is in answering the first of these questions that He replies that this present generation will not pass till the temple is destroyed and all these things connected with that be fulfilled. Other things are said in answer to the second question regarding the end of the world.

The difficulty in interpreting Matthew 24-25 is that it is dealing with two future events separated by a considerable period of time. As we explained earlier when dealing with prophetic perspective it is a bit like looking at mountain ranges in the distance. There are in fact two ranges separated by many miles but they just look like one range till you come up to them. The same thing is found with the Old Testament prophets looking into the future. They see some things connected with the first coming of Christ and some things connected with the second coming but being in the future they are somewhat mingled together. At the one time the prophets are talking of both the first coming of Christ, and also the second coming. So it is with Christ here. He is describing future events. At some points He is clearly referring to the destruction of Jerusalem and then He turns to describe the end of the world, and then He comes back to the destruction of Jerusalem again.

When Jesus says, 'This generation shall not pass, till all these things be fulfilled', He is obviously answering the first question of the disciples and referring to the destruction of the temple when not one stone would be left standing upon another. When the early Christians saw the approach of the 'abomination of desolation', the Roman army with their worship of the emperor, they heeded the words of Christ, 'Then let them which be in Judaea flee into the mountains' (v16), and they fled from the city across the Jordan to Pella and so escaped the destruction of Jerusalem. Verses 15 to 20 clearly answer the first question with regard to the destruction of Jerusalem. However, in verse 14 and verse 27 and verses 30-31 He is obviously talking of His own second coming and the end of the world. In verses 34 and 35 He returns to the temple being destroyed and is clearly referring to the events of AD70. Again, in verses 36 onwards He is talking of the end of the world.

Other passages seemingly implying an imminent return

There are some other passages of Scripture that seem to imply an imminent return of Christ. Jesus once said: 'But when they persecute you in this city, flee ye into another: for verily I say unto you, Ye shall not have gone over the cities of Israel, till the Son of man be come' (Matthew 10:23). Surely this teaches that Christ will return in the lifetime of the disciples? But this coming refers to His coming in power at His own resurrection and especially at Pentecost when He comes by His Spirit, equipping His church with His Spirit to fulfil the great commission: 'Go ye therefore, and teach all nations' (Matthew 28:19). The disciples in the time that remained for them until His death, resurrection and Pentecost will not have been able to evangelise every town in Israel. Jesus had said, 'Go not into the way of the Gentiles, and into any city of the Samaritans enter ye not: But go rather to the lost sheep of the house of Israel' (Matthew 10:5-6). The Lord in the Great Commission instructs that the gospel is to be preached to all nations, not just to the Jews (Matthew 28:18-20).

Similarly, we have the words of Christ in Mark: 'And he said unto them, Verily I say unto you, That there be some of them that stand here, which shall not taste of death, till they have seen the kingdom of God come with power'. This passage is immediately followed by the account of the transfiguration in which the veil is lifted slightly and the kingship and glory of Christ is partly revealed. But the kingdom of Christ came with power in the resurrection of Christ from the dead and, particularly, in the pouring out of the Spirit on the day of Pentecost.

Should we expect that Christ might return any day?
Jesus said His return would be as it was in the days of Noah. At that time they were eating and drinking, marrying and giving in marriage until the day that Noah entered the ark and did not realise what was happening till the flood came and carried them all away. He warns, 'Watch therefore: for ye know not what hour your Lord doth come' (Matthew 24:42). It was the same in the days of Lot: 'Likewise also as it was in the days of Lot; they did eat, they drank, they bought, they sold, they planted, they builded; but the same day that Lot went out of Sodom it rained fire and brimstone from heaven, and destroyed them all' (Luke 17:28-29). We are warned, 'Remember Lot's wife' (v32). The Lord Jesus will come as a thief in the night: 'Therefore be ye also ready: for in such an hour as ye think not the Son of man cometh' (Matthew 24:44). Christ of course can come in two ways, either by death calling us away to our long home, or in the second coming ushering in the resurrection and the final judgment.

Paul speaks clearly of Christ's return: 'But of the times and the seasons, brethren, ye have no need that I write unto you. For yourselves know perfectly that the day of the Lord so cometh as a thief in the night. For when they shall say, Peace and safety; then sudden destruction cometh upon them, as travail upon a woman with child; and they shall not escape. But ye, brethren, are not in darkness, that that day should overtake you as a thief' (1 Thessalonians 5:1-4). He had often referred to Christ's return. The Thessalonians were aware of it. They should not be sleeping but watching for the return of the Lord. The day of the Lord, that is the day of His return and judgment, will come suddenly and take many by surprise.

Peter too explained what was going to happen and warned, 'But the day of the Lord will come as a thief in the night; in the which the heavens shall pass away with a great noise, and the elements shall melt with fervent heat, the earth also and the works that are therein shall be burned up. Seeing then that all these things shall be dissolved, what manner of persons ought

EVENTS PRECEDING THE SECOND COMING

ye to be in all holy conversation and godliness, looking for and hasting unto the coming of the day of God?' (2 Peter 3:10-12). Again, the emphasis is upon the suddenness of Christ's return, but we are also to be looking forward to it and praying for Christ to come soon.

The last words of the book of Revelation, which are the very last words of the Bible, are also relevant and describe an imminent return: 'He which testifieth these things saith, Surely I come quickly. Amen. Even so, come, Lord Jesus. The grace of our Lord Jesus Christ be with you all. Amen' (Revelation 22:20-21). Christ Himself assures us that He will soon return. True, two thousand years have already passed but to God a thousand years are as one day, so His coming will be soon.

But are there events which must occur first?

Some Christians think each day they awake that this might be the day Christ returns. Should we be like them, living constantly looking for Jesus to appear? We certainly should be watching and praying each day, and be ready. Even if Christ does not return today, this very day could be our last in this world. We are to be ready for Heaven.

It does seem however that this attitude can be wrong. It can lead to extremes. The Thessalonian church, for example, was troubled that 'the day of Christ is at hand' (2 Thessalonians 2:2). As a result of this teaching some had given up their ordinary employments and were just waiting for the end of the world. But Paul is not pleased. He writes: 'Let no man deceive you by any means: for that day shall not come, except there come a falling away first, and that man of sin be revealed, the son of perdition' (2 Thessalonians 2:3). Later in the same epistle he warns those who had given up their jobs, 'For even when we were with you, this we commanded you, that if any would not work, neither should he eat. For we hear that there are some which walk among you disorderly, working not at all, but are busybodies. Now them that are such we command and exhort by our Lord Jesus Christ, that with quietness they work, and eat their own bread' (2 Thessalonians 3:10-12). It is plain from this, therefore, that certain things had to happen before Christ could return. Here we are told about the falling away which had to take place first and the revelation of the 'man of sin' or the antichrist. In Romans 11 we are told of something else which must happen before Christ returns, the conversion of the Jews to Christ. Now of course these events could take place quickly, but from this it appears that Christ could not return today.

Signs of the end

Jesus was asked the question, 'What shall be the sign of thy coming and of the end of the world?' (Matthew 24:3). A list of signs is given. There will be many deceivers, false prophets, and false Christs. There will be wars and rumours of wars. There will be famines, pestilences (plagues), and earthquakes in many places. Christians will be tortured, and killed and hated by all nations for the sake of their relationship to Christ. Many will be offended, turning away from the faith and even betraying fellow-Christians. Many will apostatise. The gospel will be preached to all nations. There shall be great tribulation (Matthew 24:4-28). These things must happen first before the end of the world, but these things have already occurred. Perhaps they will happen in a more extreme way in the future.

We have made reference already to the antichrist, or man of sin who, Paul said, was not yet revealed in his day. John also tells of an antichrist and many antichrists: 'Little children, it is the last time: and as ye have heard that antichrist shall come, even now are there many antichrists; whereby we know that it is the last time. They went out from us, but they were not of us; for if they had been of us, they would no doubt have continued with us: but they went out, that they might be made manifest that they were not all of us' (1 John 2:18-19). Antichrists were already there in the days of John but there is the great antichrist ahead. In Daniel 7 we are told about the little horn displacing three other kings also symbolised by horns: 'And of the other which came up, and before whom three fell; even of that horn that had eyes, and a mouth that spake very great things, whose look was more stout than his fellows. I beheld, and the same horn made war with the saints, and prevailed against them; until the Ancient of days came' (Daniel 7:20-22). 'And he shall speak great words against the most High, and shall wear out the saints of the most High, and think to change times and laws: and they shall be given into his hand until a time and times and the dividing of time. But the judgment shall sit, and they shall take away his dominion, to consume and to destroy it unto the end' (vv25-26). The ten horns seem to refer to the Roman emperors but three of them are displaced by the little horn which would seem to refer to the popes of Rome who took over from the emperors and continued the power of Rome and who spake great things of themselves and made huge claims but who persecuted many of the saints of the Lord. They did this especially around the time of the Reformation. Who could this be but the popes of Rome, who claimed infallibility and supremacy over the churches and the nations?

The Man of Sin

Paul tells us about the man of sin: 'Who opposeth and exalteth himself above all that is called God, or that is worshipped; so that he as God sitteth in the temple of God, shewing himself that he is God. Remember ye not, that, when I was yet with you, I told you these things? And now ye know what withholdeth that he might be revealed in his time. For the mystery of iniquity doth already work: only he who now letteth [hinders him] will let [hold him back], until he be taken out of the way. And then shall that Wicked be revealed, whom the Lord shall consume with the spirit of his mouth, and shall destroy with the brightness of his coming: Even him, whose coming is after the working of Satan with all power and signs and lying wonders, and with all deceivableness of unrighteousness in them that perish; because they received not the love of the truth, that they might be saved. And for this cause God shall send them strong delusion, that they should believe a lie' (2 Thessalonians 2:4-11).

Different interpretations have been given of this man of sin or antichrist. Some see him as a persecuting Roman emperor like Nero. Some thought it might be Napoleon or Hitler. Others think it refers to some future individual. The common view among the Reformers and Puritans is that it is the pope of Rome. For example, the *Westminster Confession of Faith* states, 'There is no other head of the church, but the Lord Jesus Christ: nor can the Pope of Rome in any sense be the head thereof, but is that antichrist, that man of sin, and son of perdition, that exalteth himself in the church against Christ, and all that is called God' (Chapter 25, Section 6). The spirit of antichrist was already at work in Paul's day and, interestingly, there is a continuity of the popes with the past, ie, with the emperors of Rome. The 'man of sin' is obviously someone within the church because he sits in the temple of God. He claims a position like God. Popes claim to be the kings of the church, wearing a crown or triple Tiara taking the position of Christ as head of the church. Rome has been notorious for its fake miracles and lying wonders. It deals in deception and those who do not love the truth of God's Word are led astray by the false teachings of the popes.

In the Book of Revelation we read of the great whore, the mother of harlots (Revelation 17) who is also a city, Babylon the great. She is drunk with the blood of the martyrs of Jesus. She is seated on a beast with seven heads. This is interpreted for us as the seven mountains on which the woman sits. Babylon was no longer a city in the first century but Rome classically is the city built upon seven hills. Peter is generally understood to be writing from Rome when he sent greetings from the local church, 'The church that is at Babylon, elected together with you, saluteth you; and so doth Marcus my son' (1 Peter 5:13). This woman is further interpreted for us as, 'that great city, which reigneth over the kings of the earth' (Revelation 17:18), and she makes war with the Lamb (v14). But she is destroyed, 'Babylon the great is fallen, is fallen, and is become the habitation of devils, and the hold of every foul spirit, and a cage of every unclean and hateful bird' (Revelation 18:2). She stands in stark contrast to the bride of Christ the new Jerusalem: 'And I John saw the holy city, new Jerusalem, coming down from God out of heaven, prepared as a bride adorned for her husband' (Revelation 21:2).

Traditionally the Reformers and Puritans saw Babylon the harlot as representing the Roman Catholic Church. Many modern Reformed theologians see it rather as representing the world in its enmity to Christ and the church. It is worth noticing however that the harlot is distinguished from the kings of the earth who committed fornication with her and the merchants of the earth who were made rich through selling their merchandise to her (Revelation 18). The Roman Catholic Church martyred many millions of godly men and women and yet claims to be the bride of Christ. The Roman Empire with its emperors which persecuted the apostles and believers in the first few centuries morphed into the Roman Catholic Church with its popes which persecuted the Reformers in later days.

These signs of the end have largely been fulfilled. The gospel is now preached to all nations. Christians are to be found in all countries. There have been famines and earthquakes and wars. There was pestilence, for example, this modern coronavirus which was troubling the whole world and the governments and scientists found great difficulty in handling it. There has been a great falling away and the love of many has grown cold. The present Pope Francis, is a Jesuit, and seems more clever and cunning than any in the past. He is even trying to get Muslims to come in under his banner in a one world church in opposition to the true blood-bought children of God.

There is still however one sign that needs to be fulfilled before Christ returns and that is the conversion of the Jews, though more Jews are being converted today than ever before. We will consider this in a future chapter.

Following the conversion of the Jews there will be a falling away and a brief, spiritually-dark period: 'Satan shall be loosed out of his prison, And shall go out to deceive the nations which are in the four quarters of the earth, Gog, and Magog, to gather them together to battle: the number of whom is as the sand of the sea. And they went up on the breadth of the earth, and compassed the camp of the saints about, and the beloved city: and fire came down from God out of heaven, and devoured them' (Revelation 20:7-9). There will be intense persecution and the very existence of the church on earth will be threatened. This will be the so-called battle of Armageddon. Then, at the point when the darkness is greatest, the Lord will return. He will judge all mankind and will cast the

THE GLORIOUS FUTURE

devil and his angels into the lake of fire and all those who side with him. He will receive His children into Heaven to glorify and enjoy Him forevermore.

CHAPTER 4

INTERPRETING THE BOOK OF REVELATION

Approaches to Interpretation
The Book of Revelation has proved mysterious to many. Its language and imagery are graphic. It is quite different from the other books of the New Testament, though similar apocalyptic language is to be found in the Old Testament, for example in sections of Ezekiel and Daniel. Some theologians and commentators avoid Revelation because of the special difficulty of interpreting it. John Calvin provided no commentary on it. However, it is in Scripture for a purpose and, indeed, when properly approached, it can provide great encouragement to every Christian, especially in difficult days and times of persecution.

There are essentially four different approaches to interpreting this book.

(1) **Preterist View**: This approach takes the Book of Revelation to be describing past events. Everything in the book happened, Preterists argue, in the first century AD. The destruction of Jerusalem features prominently. They say the writer was concerned about the evil of the Roman Empire and its persecution of the church. He uses graphic imagery to express his conviction that God will intervene to deliver His church. This type of interpretation is favoured by liberal theologians. There is, of course, some truth in this approach. A number of the passages are descriptive of events which took place in the first century. Also, it is right to ground the book firmly in the first century as a book written then, for the church as it existed at that time, as well as for us today. It is right to see the Book of Revelation as providing encouragement for the persecuted first-century believers. Confining the book to events which had taken place in the first century, however, fails to take account of the book's own testimony concerning itself at its very beginning: 'The Revelation of Jesus Christ, which God gave unto him, to shew unto his servants things which must shortly come to pass; and he sent and signified it

by his angel unto his servant John' (Revelation 1:1). Here we are clearly told that the book deals with future events.

(2) **Historicist View**: This approach sees the book as setting out a panoramic view of history from the first century till the second coming. Such commentators see it as a continuous story from John's day till the end of the world. This approach has been a common one in the Christian church down through the centuries and was followed by some of the Reformers, but there is much disagreement as to how the various episodes in church history are to be related to the book. Different interpreters, following this approach, come up with very different interpretations. The lack of consensus does not help to convince one that this approach is right. Also it tends to treat only European history and ignores the rest of the world. Again there is some truth in it, however, in so far as it lays stress upon this book as prophesying the future.

(3) **Futurist View**: The futurist view sees all of the Book of Revelation from chapter 4 onwards as referring to the end of the world. The book is not concerned with happenings in John's day or since but all of it is to do with events surrounding the return of Christ. This view is helpful in emphasising the second coming and return of Christ which are of central importance in the book, but is wrong in detaching the book completely from the present and the past.

(4) **Idealist or Poetic View**: This view emphasises that the book is concerned with encouraging persecuted believers in the first century and since then. Graphic language is used to describe in imaginative ways the triumph of God. The symbolic language is not to be taken as what will actually happen but simply a poetic way of describing the ultimate victory of Christ and His kingdom. While there is certainly truth in this overall idea and purpose, the problem again with this view is that the first verse of the book claims that it is actual prophecy of the future.

The soundest approach

None of these views, then, is entirely satisfactory, though there is a grain of truth in all of them. So how are we to interpret the book? I believe that William Hendriksen in his brief commentary entitled, *More than Conquerors*, helps us greatly in interpreting Revelation. I do not follow all his interpretations, but his general outline is very helpful. He begins by seeing the book as written to encourage first-century Christians who were suffering severe persecution and of course to encourage the rest of us in similar circumstances in the following centuries. In this he partially follows the Preterists seeing some of the events as actually having taken place even before John wrote. He follows the idealists in seeing it as a book to encourage, not simply to reveal secrets. He appreciates the historicists with their emphasis on history foretold and the futurists with their stress on the second coming. However, essentially he sees the book as consisting of seven sections which are parallel. with each of them spanning the New Testament dispensation from the first to the second coming of Christ. The symbolism of numbers is very important in the book and seven is the perfect number and the number of the church. Much of the language is of course figurative and characteristically apocalyptic and should not be taken literally. We shall now look briefly at the book and notice its various sections.

Section 1, Chapters 1-3
This section describes Christ in the midst of the seven golden lampstands which represent the church. Christ is presented in His exalted glory as the King and Head of the church and actively involved in ruling and defending it. The seven churches in Asia were indeed real churches in first century Asia Minor. However, they are also representative of churches in all ages till the return of Christ. Seven, as we noticed is the complete and perfect number and the number of the church. These letters are highly relevant for the churches of today, both rebuking the evil in the church and encouraging the churches to be faithful and stand for Christ and the truth.

Section 2, Chapters 4-7
This section describes the book with the seven seals. First, we are given a vision into Heaven and there we see the Throne that rules Heaven and earth. What an encouragement this is when there are powerful persecuting forces! God reigns, let the earth be glad (Psalm 97:1). Then a scroll is pictured in the hand of God on the throne and this scroll obviously

contains the purposes of God with regard to the world and especially His church. Initially, none is found worthy to open the book but then the Lion of the tribe of Judah steps forward, takes the book and opens the seals. This Lion is none other than Christ, the Lamb of God who was slain to take away the sins of the world. He appears like 'a lamb as it had been slain' (Revelation 5:6), so this takes us right back to Calvary. The opening of the seals is the unfolding of God's purposes, or the rule of Christ in the New Testament dispensation. He shall rule till His enemies be made His footstool. This section ends with the church of God saved and at rest and peace in Heaven: 'These are they which came out of great tribulation, and have washed their robes, and made them white in the blood of the Lamb. Therefore are they before the throne of God, and serve him day and night in his temple: and he that sitteth on the throne shall dwell among them. They shall hunger no more, neither thirst any more; neither shall the sun light on them, nor any heat. For the Lamb which is in the midst of the throne shall feed them, and shall lead them unto living fountains of waters: and God shall wipe away all tears from their eyes' (Revelation 7:14-17).

Section 3, Chapters 8-11
This section describes the seven trumpets of judgment. The previous section described the tribulations through which God's people pass in this world. The seals of trial and persecution render necessary the trumpets of judgment. In answer to the prayers of the suffering church, God sends down through the centuries, His plagues on land, sea and air. So again this section parallels the previous one. The prayers of the godly, offered with incense from the altar of Christ's sufferings, are heard, and their persecutors are punished. Christ is ruling, restraining and conquering all His and our enemies. Again, the end point is the final judgment: 'And the nations were angry, and thy wrath is come, and the time of the dead, that they should be judged, and that thou shouldest give reward unto thy servants the prophets, and to the saints, and them that fear thy name, small and great; and shouldest destroy them which destroy the earth' (Revelation 11:18).

Section 4, Chapters 12-14
The first half of Revelation that we have just looked at, describes the struggle of the church on earth, how it is persecuted and how it is avenged, protected and victorious. This second half of Revelation, to which we now turn, describes the deeper, spiritual background. Christ and His church are persecuted by Satan and his allies. This section, chapters 12-14, describes how the woman and the man-Child are persecuted by the dragon and his helpers. The birth of the man-Child obviously refers to Christ being born, so this takes us back to the beginning of the New Testament age. The child Christ ascends to Heaven but the dragon makes war with the woman and her seed, which is of course the church. Christ and His church are persecuted by the dragon representing Satan.

With regard to the beasts of Chapter 13, I would deviate somewhat from Hendriksen and follow the traditional Reformed interpretation which sees the beasts representing antichrist. The first arises out of the sea which is representative of the nations, a fearful persecuting beast and having the characteristics of a leopard, a bear and a lion. This would seem to represent the Roman Empire which terribly persecuted the early church. It should also be seen as those persecuting governments of today. The beast from the earth is represented as looking like a lamb with two horns and speaking like a dragon. This appears to represent the papacy. The Pope claimed to be in the place of Christ who is the Lamb of God. He pretends to be gentle but speaks like a dragon, arrogantly claiming to be the mouthpiece of God and infallible as he speaks *ex cathedra*. He too and his false church persecuted the true children of God who suffered greatly at the hand of this false lamb. The popes of Rome have the blood of many thousands of godly men and women on their hands. One thinks of the cruelty to the Waldensians, the inquisition in Spain and the Netherlands, Saint Bartholomew's day massacre in France and Bloody Mary's persecution in England, to mention just a few.

This is the same individual as the little horn of Daniel 7:8. The number of the true church is seven but the number of the church of antichrist is six (given as 666 in Revelation 13:18). It is short of seven and is defective and something that is vital is missing. Babylon is fallen (Revelation 14:8). She is the church of the antichrist and the opposite of new Jerusalem. Again, this section ends with the judgment of the wicked, the followers of the beasts and of the dragon, at the end of world history: 'And the angel thrust in his sickle into the earth, and gathered the vine of the earth, and cast it into the great winepress of the wrath of God. And the winepress was trodden without the city, and blood came out of the winepress, even unto the horse bridles, by the space of a thousand and six hundred furlongs' (Revelation 14:19-20). As followers of Christ, we are on the winning side, despite fiery trials and persecution.

Section 5, Chapters 15-16

This section describes the seven vials or bowls of wrath poured out upon the followers of the dragon and the beasts. It parallels the opening of the seven seals of trials and the sounding of the seven trumpets of judgment. This section describes what will happen to those who persist in rejecting the gospel. On them will be poured the seven last plagues of God's wrath.

First, we are told of the sea of glass and those who are victorious over the dragon and the beasts. The picture here is drawn from the Israelites at the Red Sea having had victory over the Egyptians and singing the Song of Moses (Exodus 15) in triumph. Now, 'They sing the song of Moses the servant of God, and the song of the Lamb, saying, Great and marvellous are thy works, Lord God Almighty; just and true are thy ways, thou King of saints. Who shall not fear thee, O Lord, and glorify thy name?' (Revelation 15:3-4). The vials of wrath are poured upon the earth, the sea, the rivers, the sun, the seat of the beast, etc. All who reject the light of the gospel will perish. The nations gather against the true church to destroy it in the great battle of Armageddon, but Christ returns to deliver His people in the second coming and final judgment. We are told that 'the cities of the nations fell: and great Babylon came in remembrance before God, to give unto her the cup of the wine of the fierceness of his wrath. And every island fled away, and the mountains were not found' (Revelation 16:19-20). Again, the end note is God's wrath upon the apostates. The plagues which come upon them are exceeding great, much worse than those on Egypt.

Section 6, Chapters 17-19

This section describes the fall of the great harlot Babylon and the beasts. Chapter 17 describes the woman arrayed in purple and scarlet and decked with gold and precious stones having 'a golden cup in her hand full of abominations and filthiness of her fornication' (v4). This Babylon the Great, drunk with the blood of saints, rides on a beast full of the names of blasphemy having seven heads and ten horns. The seven heads are interpreted as the seven hills on which the city is built, obviously a reference to Rome. The ten horns are ten kings who reign with the beast. They make war on the Lamb. We think of how the emperors of Rome set themselves against the Christian church. Later the Roman Popes took the place of the emperors and persecuted the true children of God, especially at the time of the Reformation and following that. Many modern Reformed commentators like Hendriksen interpret this great city as the world in its opposition to the church. The world is pleasure-mad, luxurious, arrogant, and the centre of anti-Christian culture and persecution. However, I believe, with the majority of Reformers and Reformed theologians before the twentieth century, that it is better to see Babylon as the false church dominated by the Roman Catholic antichrist, the pretend bride of Christ, that deceives many with her sacraments, claims infallibility, her pretensions to be able to forgive sins, and assertions that there is salvation for no-one but those within its membership. The Roman Catholic Church has cruelly persecuted the true saints of God for centuries and would still do it today if she had the power. If Babylon is equated with the world it is difficult to distinguish it as a city from those who mourn over its fall, that is, the kings of the earth and the merchants. If Babylon the Great is equated with the Roman Catholic Church it is easy to see how its fall causes sorrow to those who obtained their wealth and power through trading with it. It is an institution of vast wealth and influence right up to the present day. The whore stands in stark contrast to the bride of Christ. If the New Jerusalem, the Bride of Christ, is a church why should the harlot, or false bride, not be the false church? Then Christ appears: 'And I saw heaven opened, and behold a white horse; and he that sat upon him was called Faithful and True, and in righteousness he doth judge and make war. His eyes were as a flame of fire, and on his head were many crowns; and he had a name written, that no man knew, but he himself. And he was clothed with a vesture dipped in blood: and his name is called The Word of God. And the armies which were in heaven followed him upon white horses, clothed in fine linen, white and clean. And out of his mouth goeth a sharp sword, that with it he should smite the nations: and he shall rule them with a rod of iron: and he treadeth the winepress of the fierceness and wrath of Almighty God' (Revelation 19:11-15). War against the Lamb and His followers is doomed to failure. The beast and the false prophet and those who receive the mark of the beast, that is the followers of the beast, are cast into the lake of fire. Christ and His church will always win.

Section 7, Chapters 20-22
This section deals with the locking up of Satan in the bottomless pit and later with the judgment of Satan and of all mankind. It covers the account of the final state, the appearance of the New Jerusalem, and the new heaven and the new earth.

Revelation 20 – Its importance
This chapter is important because we find here reference to the thousand years or the millennium around which various eschatological views have arisen and so we must devote more time to it. Essentially there are three views though obviously there are many variations of these three views:

> (1) **Premillennialism** is the understanding that Christ will one day return to reign on this earth as a literal, human King in Jerusalem and His reign will last for 1000 years. This view was common in the early church when it had the name Chiliasm. It was revived by the Anabaptists at the time of the Reformation. It became popular among some in the nineteenth century due to the teaching of Edward Irving (1792-1834). Dispensationalism, which is also Premillennial in its understanding of prophecy, became the view of the Christian Brethren and the Fundamentalists of America, and would

predominate in Evangelical circles in the twentieth century due particularly to its being popularised by the *Scofield Reference Bible* and by radio and TV evangelists. We will look at this view in more detail in a later chapter.

(2) **Postmillennialism** is the view that there will be in the future a prolonged period of great spiritual prosperity for the church of Christ which would be equated with the thousand years, though it is not to be taken literally as being one thousand years. After the blessed millennium there will be a falling away spiritually and a time of fierce persecution and then Christ will return. So the return of Christ is after the millennium. This view was common among the English and Dutch Puritans and the early Scottish and American theologians. It would be the position held by Jonathan Edwards, the Hodges, the Alexanders and B. B. Warfield and many others of the classical Reformed theologians.

(3) **Amillennialism** is the view that there is no millennium or rather that the whole New Testament age is to be seen as the millennium. This would be the commonest view held today by Reformed theologians. This view was promoted by Dutch and Dutch American theologians of the twentieth century such as Herman Bavinck, Louis Berkhof and William Hendriksen. It tends to be pessimistic in outlook, expecting things to get worse and worse till Christ returns, which could be very soon. It would seem to have been influenced somewhat by the drastic effects on the churches of higher criticism, evolutionary thinking and rationalism, ideas and theories which have taken over and destroyed all the mainline churches in the West, and was further exacerbated by two devastating world wars. These things have undermined the optimism of many modern Christians who fail to see how a golden age of blessing could possibly come.

Revelation 20 – An Exposition

Revelation 20 begins with an angel binding the dragon, the old serpent, obviously a reference to the one who deceived Eve in the garden of Eden. To make it completely clear, we are told that the one bound was the devil and Satan. The angel has a key and a great chain and binds Satan for 1000 years. Further we are told that he cast him into the bottomless pit and shut him up, obviously with the key, and set a seal upon him in the pit so that he could deceive the nations no more till the 1000 years be fulfilled, and then he must be released for a little time. Some take the language in Revelation literally but we must be cautious in doing that since much of the language is obviously symbolic. You cannot, for example, tie a spirit with a chain. It requires a body for someone to be chained and the devil has no body. The chain, the lock and the seal are pictures, and also, the thousand years should simply be viewed as a long period of time.

The question arises as to when this was done, or when it will be done. Hendriksen takes us back to the gospels and sees this binding of Satan as that which Christ did on the cross. He refers to passages such as where Christ says, 'No man can enter into a strong man's house, and spoil his goods, except he will first bind the strong man; and then he will spoil his house' (Mark 3:27). He sees Christ as the one who bound Satan so that the gospel can be preached to everyone and Satan's kingdom plundered. Before the death of Christ, the whole world lay in heathen darkness apart from the tiny land of Israel. Following Christ's ascension came the day of Pentecost and the rapid missionary expansion of the church of Christ across the Roman world.

This position is sane and sensible and much can be said in its favour. There are however a few problems. This passage in Revelation 20 states that the devil was locked up and sealed in the bottomless pit, therefore unable to move around this world, deceiving the nations, yet Peter states plainly, 'Be sober, be vigilant; because your adversary the devil, as a roaring lion, walketh about, seeking whom he may devour' (1 Peter 5:8). Surely Satan cannot be both locked up and be walking around devouring people? We are told that he was unable to deceive the nations yet Christ warns that if it were possible the very elect would be deceived (Matthew 24:24). Paul warns us of the need for the shield of faith to quench the fiery darts of the wicked one [i.e., the dragon] (Ephesians 6:16). We look around the world today and we see billions of men and women deceived by the devil following Islam, Buddhism, Hinduism, Atheism and Roman Catholicism. We are reminded of what John states in his first letter: 'We know we are of God, and the whole world lieth in wickedness [or, under the sway, or power, of the wicked one]' (1 John 5:19. In this verse the Greek *ponero* is better translated 'wicked one', or 'evil one', i.e. Satan, rather than the impersonal term, 'wickedness'). Again, surely evolution is a great deception of Satan and yet how widely it is accepted. Amillennial theologians will argue that the situation is much better than in Old Testament times and that of course is true though more than half the world was in just as much darkness for 1500 years after the death of Christ as it was before.

A further problem is that the passage specifically states that before the end Satan will be loosed for a little season. If he was bound by the great historical-redemptive act of Christ on Calvary, how can he be loosed without undoing the victory of Christ on the cross? Surely Christ's death is a once-for-all crushing of the serpent's head? For those who follow the Amillennial interpretation they explain it as things getting really bad before the end. But it has been really bad many times in the past with Muslim persecution and Roman Catholic persecution. How could it possibly get worse?

A case for Postmillennialism

In the Postmillennial understanding this millennium is in the future and coincides with the promises of an age of great blessing foretold in the Old Testament, for example in Psalm 72 where it is said of Christ: 'He shall have dominion also from sea to sea, and from the river unto the ends of the earth. They that dwell in the wilderness shall bow before him; and his enemies shall lick the dust. The kings of Tarshish and of the isles shall bring presents: the kings of Sheba and Seba shall offer gifts. Yea, all kings shall fall down before him: all nations shall serve him' (Psalm 72:8-11). This has never happened up till now. This future millennium would also involve the conversion of the Jews described in Romans 11 and the resulting 'life from the dead' (Romans 11:15) for the Gentile world.

Let us look further at how Postmillennialists understand Revelation 20. Verses 1 and 2 tell of a future day when Heaven will intervene in the history of the world and Satan will be greatly restrained and restricted. His ability to deceive will be hugely reduced. False religions will largely disappear, liberal theology will have little appeal and evolution will be seen as nonsense. Christ was enthroned in Heaven at His ascension and reigns over the earth, but now His enemies will clearly be seen to be His footstool. The gospel will be preached with power and multitudes will be saved. During this period of triumph the martyrs who died for the cause of Christ will reign with Him in the sense that they will be seen universally to have been on the right side and the winning side. There will be a spiritual resurrection, 'a life from the dead' for the church which for so long has been struggling against atheism, unbelief and heresy. The second death of eternal Hell will have no power over the true Christians. The Lord's people will be priests and kings in the spiritual sense. But then at the end of this period Satan will be loosed, deceive the nations again and stir up intense persecution against the true people of God. When it seems that the church is about to be exterminated, Christ will return and destroy His enemies. The great white throne will be set up and the final judgment will take place.

This was the classical Protestant understanding of the passage. However, we must not be too dogmatic. Prophecy is notoriously difficult to interpret. God often takes us by surprise. One thing we must understand is that there will never be shortcuts to salvation. The way to be saved is always the same. Jesus said: 'You must be born again'. Paul responded to the question of the Philippian jailor, 'What must I do to be saved?' with the clear answer, 'Believe on the Lord Jesus Christ, and thou shalt be saved, and thy house' (Acts 16:30-31). Every individual, whether Jew or Gentile, must repent and believe the gospel to be saved.

The Book of Revelation reveals, as William Hendriksen rightly states, that Christians are 'more than conquerors'. Chapters 20-22 declare complete victory for Christ and His church and the destruction of all His enemies including that dragon, Satan. It tells of the blessed future of Christians and the fearful lake of fire awaiting unbelievers.

CHAPTER 5

THE JEWS

There is one matter which it is very important for us to consider when thinking of events which must occur before Christ can return. Many Christians believe that the Jews as a people will one day be converted to believe in Jesus as their Messiah. There is a special New Testament passage which it is vital for us to understand when thinking of the future and that is Romans 11. We believe that God here makes great promises concerning the Jews which are yet to be fulfilled. Paul's epistle to the Romans is the most theological of all the epistles and sets out clearly many of the great truths of the Christian faith.

Romans 1-8
In Romans chapter 1 Paul makes a great statement which in a way sets out the theme of this Epistle and declares what it is all about: 'For I am not ashamed of the gospel of Christ: for it is the power of God unto salvation to every one that believeth; to the Jew first, and also to the Greek. For therein is the righteousness of God revealed from faith to faith: as it is written, The just shall live by faith' (Romans 1:16-17). It is worth noticing in passing how we are told here that the gospel is to the Jew first. Many Christians today believe in what is called Replacement Theology. This is the idea that all the promises of the Old Testament in connection with the Jews belong now to the church. For them the church has replaced Israel and is the new Israel. They believe that with the crucifixion of Christ the Jews lost the special position they once had. While this is largely the case, it is not the full story. We must be careful lest we oversimplify the teaching of Scripture. We see here that, in writing to the church in Rome, Paul asserts that the Jews still have a special priority. The gospel is 'to the Jew first'. Wherever Paul went in his missionary journeys he first went to the

Jews and to the synagogue with the good news and only when they rejected the message did he turn to the Gentiles. For example, when he was brought as a prisoner to Rome he explained the gospel first to the Jews and only when the majority of them rejected the gospel did he turn to the Gentiles warning the Jews, 'Be it known therefore unto you, that the salvation of God is sent unto the Gentiles, and that they will hear it' (Acts 28:28).

Paul proceeds in the rest of Romans 1 to show the sins of the Gentiles who did not have the Old Testament which contains the law of God. On them the wrath of God rested. In chapter 2 he demonstrates the sinfulness of the Jews who did have the law. In chapter 3 he concludes that both Jews and Gentiles are guilty before God and need salvation. In the second part of chapter 3 he presents Jesus Christ as the needed Saviour, the One who atones for our sins. In Chapters 4 and 5 he declares that justification is by faith alone in Christ alone. In chapters 6 to 8 he deals with sanctification and assurance. Then in chapters 9-11 he explains election and God's sovereignty in salvation, and this is the section on which we must especially focus.

Romans 9

In Romans chapter 9 Paul writes of his great love to his fellow Jews and his sadness at the way they have generally rejected Christ. He could wish himself lost if only the Jews were saved. He speaks of the wonderful privileges they had, 'the adoption, and the glory, and the covenants, and the giving of the law, and the service of God, and the promises' etc (Romans 9:4). But not all Jews are lost. Election is very important. God chose Isaac but not Ishmael. Rebecca had twins but God's election was shown in that even before they were born, or had done good or evil, it was said to her, 'The elder shall serve the younger' (v12). And so it is written: 'Jacob have I loved, but Esau have I hated' (v13). The potter has power over the clay to make whatever type of vessel he wishes. God could show mercy to all, or to none, but rather chose to save some: 'Therefore hath he mercy on whom he will have mercy, and whom he will he hardeneth' (v18). Though Israel were largely a rebellious people God always had His elect among them:

'Though the number of the children of Israel be as the sand of the sea, a remnant shall be saved' (v27).

Romans 10

In chapter 10 Paul continues to speak of his love for his fellow Jews: 'Brethren, my heart's desire and prayer to God for Israel is, that they might be saved. For I bear them record that they have a zeal of God, but not according to knowledge' (Romans 10:1-2). Israel here cannot possibly mean the church. He is referring to his kinsmen, the Jews, who are zealous in seeking to save themselves but, wrongly, as it is by works. He explains the way of salvation is by faith alone. He notes that Israel are still rejecting the gospel as Isaiah had prophesied they would: 'But to Israel he saith, All day long I have stretched forth my hands unto a disobedient and gainsaying people' (10:21).

Romans 11

Paul begins Romans 11 by asking if God had completely rejected the Jews and notes that that cannot be the case because he himself, a Jew, is saved. He asserts that God did not cast away His people whom He foreknew and fore-loved. Israel had, and have a special place in God's election. He is aware that there is a godly remnant just as was the case in the days of Elijah: 'Even so then at this present time also there is a remnant according to the election of grace' (11:5). Being a mere Israelite will save no one. It never did and never will, but election saves and the rest were blinded (v7).

The Apostle then asks a critical question in verse 11. Have the Jews stumbled so that they will totally fall away? He answers in a strong negative but proceeds to make an important point: 'Rather through their fall salvation is come unto the Gentiles, for to provoke them to jealousy' (v11). In a strange way the Jews' rejection of the gospel meant that God turned from them to the despised Gentiles in order to provoke the Jews to jealousy for their soul's salvation. Then a most important statement is made: 'Now if the fall of them be the riches of the world, and the diminishing of them the riches of the Gentiles; how much more their fulness?' (v12). If, as was the case, the falling away of the Jews was a blessing to the Gentiles, how much more will their fullness and restoration be a blessing? Right through this section of the Epistle, Paul is obviously using the term 'Israel' and the term 'Jews' to describe ethnic Israel and not the church. Paul proceeds to make a great promise, 'For if the casting away of them be the reconciling of the world, what shall the receiving of them be, but life from the dead?' (v15). Paul's argument runs as follows: If the rejecting of Jesus by the Jews brought salvation to many Gentiles, surely then the salvation of the Jews will bring a great blessing, a massive revival, 'life from the dead', to the Gentile church.

The Olive Tree

The Apostle next describes the church as being like an olive tree. The root grew in Old Testament times. The root is holy and so the branches, which though originally pagan Gentiles, are also holy. The Gentiles are like a wild olive tree some branches of which were cut from it and grafted into the good olive tree. Indeed, Jewish branches were broken off the good olive tree so as to allow this to happen. The Gentiles, however, are warned against pride: 'But if thou boast, thou bearest not the root, but the root thee. Thou wilt say then, The branches were broken off, that I might be grafted in. Well; because of unbelief they were broken off, and thou standest by faith. Be not high-minded, but fear: for if God spared not the natural branches, take heed lest he also spare not thee' (vv18-21).

The Gentiles have nothing to be proud of and are warned that they too can be broken off and rejected. Paul encourages the unbelieving Jews that they should not despair, but repent and believe and they will be saved: 'And they also, if they abide not still in unbelief, shall be grafted in: for God is able to graft them in again. For if thou wert cut out of the olive tree which is wild by nature, and wert grafted contrary to nature into a good olive tree: how much more shall these, which be the natural branches, be grafted into their own olive tree?' (vv23-24).

THE JEWS

'All Israel'
The next verse (v25) is crucial in the argument of the Apostle: 'For I would not, brethren, that ye should be ignorant of this mystery, lest ye should be wise in your own conceits; that blindness in part is happened to Israel, until the fullness of the Gentiles be come in' (v25). A 'mystery' in the New Testament is a secret hidden from past generations but now revealed. In Old Testament times salvation was largely restricted to the Jews, but now something wonderful has happened. Blindness in part has happened to the Jews. God in His sovereignty and justice has blinded them so that they cannot see that Jesus is the Messiah. Thankfully it has only been in part and there have been Jews like Peter and Paul who have been saved and indeed down through the centuries since the apostles there have always been a few Jewish converts. The Jews, as a whole, rejected Jesus and God has instead filled His church with Gentiles. There is here, however, that important word 'until'. The blindness which has come upon the Jews is only 'until the fullness of the Gentiles be come in'. The Apostle envisages a day coming when this will change. When the fullness of the Gentiles will have been brought in, a large number of them being converted, then something new will happen: 'And so all Israel shall be saved' (v26).

At this point many commentators suddenly and inexplicably take 'Israel' to mean the church composed of Gentiles and a few Jews when in all the other references in Romans 9-11 'Israel' clearly refers to ethnic Israel. Surely this is bad exegesis though very common? Unless there is an overwhelming reason for it, 'Israel' should be taken to mean what it means in the rest of the chapter. Here there is a clear prophecy that so many of the Jews will be saved that it can be said that 'all Israel shall be saved.' Just as it was previously said that they, Israel, had been cast away (v1) although a remnant was saved, so now it is said that all Israel shall be saved. That does not of course imply that every individual Israelite will be saved, but rather Israel as a whole. It is also important to emphasise that they can only be saved by exercising faith in Christ. They will not continue in unbelief. There is only one way of salvation for Jew and Gentile. As the Scripture says, 'There shall come out of Sion the Deliverer, and shall turn away ungodliness from Jacob' (v26). This Deliverer is the Lord Jesus who by His Spirit turns sinners from their ungodliness, granting repentance now at last to the Jews, indeed the majority of Jews, as well as to Gentiles.

Beloved for their fathers' sake

The same theme is continued in the next verse (v27) and the 'them' referred to in that verse as well as the 'enemies' of the following verse can obviously refer to none but the ethnic Jews: 'For this is my covenant unto them, when I shall take away their sins. As concerning the gospel, they are enemies for your sakes: but as touching the election, they are beloved for the fathers' sakes' (vv27-28). Why give 'Israel' in verse 26 a different meaning from the 'them' and the 'enemies' of verses 27 and 28? God made His covenant with Abraham and it is a covenant of grace, all of grace and therefore an eternal covenant. Similarly, God's covenant with Moses and Israel was a covenant of grace. Yes, the Jews were cast away for a time but then God returns to them. They still have a place in God's plan of election. The Jews became enemies in order that the gospel might reach the Gentiles, but God's election remains. Israel is beloved for their fathers' sakes (v28). God still has a purpose of mercy for the Jews. Verse 29 is wonderfully reassuring: 'For the gifts and calling of God are without repentance'. God bestowed His gifts and calling upon Israelites and they are still unique in His eyes. He hardened them for a time because of their unbelief but they are still special to Him. Here He is promising the restoration of Israel to a central place in His church.

A Future Day

Paul explains that the Gentiles in Rome were enemies in the past because of their unbelief in God, but now they have obtained mercy through the Jews' unbelief, 'Even so have these also now not believed, that through your mercy they also may obtain mercy' (v31). We are to have a special concern and love in our hearts for the Jews and particularly to seek their salvation. Thinking of these things and looking forward to the day when his kinsmen according to the flesh will be grafted in again to the olive tree of the church, Paul breaks out into a doxology: 'O the depth of the riches both of the wisdom and knowledge of God! how unsearchable are his judgments, and his ways past finding out! For who hath known the mind of the Lord? or who hath been his counsellor? Or who hath first given to him, and it shall be recompensed unto him again? For of him, and through him, and to him, are all things: to whom be glory for ever. Amen' (vv33-36). God is working out His plan of salvation and God still has a great purpose for the Jews. Although the Apostle grieves that for the time being the Jews are unbelievers, it fills his heart with joy to think of that future day when the Jews as a people will be converted and accept the true Messiah.

Not all Reformed theologians would agree with this interpretation of Romans 11. For example, Stuart Olyott in his commentary on Romans (*The Gospel as it Really is*) argues that there are no special promises for the Jews. In his classic *Systematic Theology*, Louis Berkhof writes of Christ that 'He does not hint at any prospective restoration and conversion of the Jewish people' (page 699). Is that really true? In point of fact there are several passages where Jesus indicates that there will be a blessed day ahead for the Jews. For example, our Lord does say, 'Jerusalem shall be trodden down of the Gentiles, until the times of the Gentiles be fulfilled' (Luke 21:24). The 'until' clearly implies that there is a time coming when Jerusalem will no longer be trodden underfoot by the Gentiles. It implies that there is a time of blessing coming for Jerusalem and the Jews.

Another important statement of Jesus also implies the conversion of the Jews. Jesus mourns over the Jews and weeps over the judgment coming upon them for rejecting Him but also speaks of a coming day when their attitude will be totally different: 'O Jerusalem, Jerusalem, thou that killest the prophets, and stonest them which are sent unto thee, how often would I have gathered thy children together, even as a hen gathereth her chickens under her wings, and ye would not! Behold, your house is left unto you desolate. For I say unto you, Ye shall not see me henceforth, till ye shall say, Blessed is he that cometh in the name of the Lord' (Matthew 23:37-39). Here Jesus is looking forward to the conversion of the Jews and the day that they will bless Him. He will not return again until the majority of Jews will repent and believe and rejoice in His coming.

While it is true that at present, 'Strait is the gate, and narrow is the way, which leadeth unto life, and few there be that find it' (Matthew 7:14), many of His parables speak of better days ahead. In the parable of the leaven, Christ speaks of the kingdom spreading till the whole world is leavened or Christianised. The parable of the mustard seed implies that the church will not remain a tiny minority but become a great tree so that the birds of the air will come and dwell in its branches. Jesus compares the Jews to a fig tree, planted in a vineyard. The owner comes to the gardener saying, 'Behold, these three years I come seeking fruit on this fig tree, and find none: cut it down; why cumbereth it the ground?' (Luke 13:7). For three years Christ laboured among the Jews, but there was little fruit. 'And he answering said unto him, Lord, let it alone this year also, till I shall dig about it, and dung it: And if it bear fruit, well: and if not, then after that thou shalt cut it down' (vv8-9). Christ the Mediator intercedes for the Jewish fig tree. It was spared till AD70, and many Jews were saved but the general rejection of the Messiah continued till eventually it was cut down. However the stump remained in the ground, like Nebuchadnezzar's stump (Daniel 4). Jesus makes reference again to the fig tree when talking about the events preceding His second coming: 'Now learn a parable of the fig tree; When his branch is yet tender, and putteth forth leaves, ye know that summer is nigh: So likewise ye, when ye shall see all these things, know that it is near, even at the doors' (Matthew 24:32-33). When the stump of God's fig tree begins again to sprout and put forth leaves, the return of Christ is approaching. Again the implication here is that the Jews will yet be saved and become a fruitful tree in the vineyard of the Lord.

Ezekiel 37

There are many Old Testament passages which can be seen to teach the restoration of Israel. One of the clearest examples is Ezekiel 37, the valley of dead bones. Here Ezekiel, the prophet, is given an amazing vision. He is taken by the Spirit of the Lord into a valley which is full of bones. He had to walk among them to be convicted of the dire reality of the situation. There were many bones and they were very dry. What a horrible sight! All these skeletons around! Then he is asked a question: 'Can these bones live?' Surely the answer is obvious. Common sense says, No. But the prophet however wisely replies: 'O Lord God, thou knowest' (v3). God says to him: 'Son of man, these bones are the whole house of Israel: behold, they say, Our bones are dried, and our hope is lost: we are cut off for our parts' (v11). Israel is in captivity in Babylon, Jerusalem is destroyed, the temple is burnt with fire and the Promised Land is empty. Israel is cut off and her hope for the future is lost.

Ezekiel is then given a strange command: 'Prophesy upon these bones, and say unto them, O ye dry bones, hear the word of the Lord. Thus saith the Lord God unto these bones; Behold, I will cause breath to enter into you, and ye shall live: And I will lay sinews upon you, and will bring up flesh upon you, and cover you with skin, and put breath in you, and ye shall live; and ye shall know that I am the Lord' (vv4-6). The prophet is to proclaim God's word to the heaps of bones.

As Ezekiel was prophesying we are told, 'There was a noise, and behold a shaking, and the bones came together, bone to his bone. And when I beheld, lo, the sinews and the flesh came up upon them, and the skin covered them above: but there was no breath in them' (vv7-8). What a remarkable, indeed hair-raising sight, that must have been! All round the valley bones were moving, finding other bones, sinews and flesh growing on them and skin covering the bodies, so that now there was a valley full of dead bodies. So many and yet still so dead!

The prophet is now commanded: 'Prophesy unto the wind, prophesy, son of man, and say to the wind, Thus saith the Lord God; Come from the four winds, O breath, and breathe upon these slain, that they may live' (v9). Remember the word for breath, wind and spirit in Hebrew is the same, '*ruach*'. Now Ezekiel tells us: 'So I prophesied as he commanded me, and the breath came into them, and they lived, and stood up upon their feet, an exceeding great army' (v10). God's Spirit came down upon them causing a wonderful resurrection. What a sight, thousands of soldiers ready for battle!

The vision is then explained to the prophet: 'Behold, O my people, I will open your graves, and cause you to come up out of your graves, and bring you into the land of Israel. And ye shall know that I am the Lord, when I have opened your graves, O my people, and brought you up out of your graves, And shall put my spirit in you, and ye shall live, and I shall place you in your own land: then shall ye know that I the Lord have spoken it, and performed it, saith the Lord' (vv12-14). Though at that specific point in time the situation seemed hopeless, yet God was going to do great things. Israel was to be spiritually resurrected, returned to their own land and become a mighty army for God. After seventy years the Jews returned, the temple was rebuilt on a far more modest scale and eventually the walls of Jerusalem rebuilt. But it was only a few Jews who returned. Their enemies said of them, 'What do these feeble Jews?' (Nehemiah 4:2). God helped them but there is no sign of the mighty army. They struggled on dominated by the great powers around them – the Persians, the Greek Seleucids and the Romans.

How was this passage fulfilled, or how will it be fulfilled? Since the days of Ezekiel, there has been no mighty resurrection of the Jews or great army standing up for God. Replacement theologians spiritualise it and say it refers to the Christian church and yet there is a specific reference here to the Jewish people, their captivity and their land. God says, 'Behold, I will take the children of Israel from among the heathen, whither they be gone, and will gather them on every side, and bring them into their own land' (Ezekiel 37:21).

Surely no one can consider the history of the Jews over the last 2000 years and fail to see the special hand and purpose of God in that people. Pilate was reluctant to execute Jesus knowing that Jesus was innocent of the charges brought against Him by the Jews, but the Jews wanted rid of Jesus: 'Then answered all the people, and said, His blood be on us, and on our children' (Matthew 27:25). In AD70 the Romans destroyed Jerusalem and the temple. They massacred millions of Jews and sold the rest as slaves.

THE JEWS

For the next 2000 years they were hounded from country to country. They were horribly persecuted by the Roman Catholic Inquisition, subjected to vicious pogroms by the Russians, six million of them were killed by the Nazis, everywhere they were hated. Antisemitism is universally common even to this day. Yet they have survived and kept their identity. Furthermore, contrary to all historical precedent, they have been settled again in their own land and already eight million of them, or half the Jews in the world have returned to the land of Israel. There they have been surrounded by numerous and powerful, hostile armies: Egypt, Syria, Jordan, Iraq, Iran, etc, which from the day of their independence in 1948 have repeatedly attacked them, yet they have survived. And not only have they survived but now have become the superpower of the Middle East. How could this happen apart from the hand of God upon them for good?

But we are still awaiting the conversion of the Jews as a people. In 1948 there were some 30 Christian Jews in Israel. Today it is reckoned that there are some 30,000 and this number is increasing exponentially. We are looking for God to do even more. We are waiting for the Lord as it were to raise them from the dead and convert them for Himself into a mighty army to evangelise the world.

But is this idea of the conversion of the Jews an odd view held by just a few strange people? To the contrary, it was by far the commonest view of orthodox theologians from the time of the Reformation till the twentieth century. The Westminster Standards are the great standards of the Presbyterian Church, produced by the Westminster Assembly of Divines in the seventeenth century. The answer to Question 191 of the *Westminster Larger Catechism* is very informative. In dealing with the Lord's Prayer the question is asked: 'What do we pray for in the second petition?' The answer given is as follows: 'In the second petition, (which is, *Thy kingdom come,*) acknowledging ourselves and all mankind to be by nature under the dominion of sin and Satan, we pray, that the kingdom of sin and Satan may be destroyed, the gospel propagated throughout the world, the Jews called, the fullness of the Gentiles brought in; the church furnished with all gospel-officers and ordinances, purged from corruption, countenanced and maintained by the civil magistrate: that the ordinances of Christ may be purely dispensed, and made effectual to the converting of those that are yet in their sins, and the confirming, comforting, and building up of those that are already converted: that Christ would rule in our hearts here, and hasten the time of his second coming, and our reigning with him forever: and that he would be pleased so to exercise the kingdom of his power in all the world, as may best conduce to these ends.'

From this, it is plain that the Presbyterian Standards envisage the calling, the effectual calling, or conversion of the Jews and the fullness of the Gentiles which means the conversion of many Gentiles as a result flowing from the Jews' conversion. We should pray for, work for, and expect the conversion of the majority of the Jews to Christ before the second coming. It is foretold in many Old Testament passages. Zechariah, for example, wrote what God told him: 'And I will pour upon the house of David, and upon the inhabitants of Jerusalem, the spirit of grace and of supplications: and they shall look upon me whom they have pierced, and they shall mourn for him, as one mourneth for his only son, and shall be in bitterness for him, as one that is in bitterness for his firstborn' (Zechariah 12:10). Here again we have a prophecy of the Jews being converted.

CHAPTER 6

DISPENSATIONAL PREMILLENNIALISM

It is important to consider Dispensational Premillennialism, as it has been the generally held viewpoint of most evangelical churches for the last 150 years. It has been widely promoted by radio and TV ministries, by the *Scofield Reference Bible*, and by Bible institutes and colleges and by popular books like Hal Lindsey's *The Late Great Planet Earth*. Dispensationalists view the Jews' return to the land of Palestine and the setting up of the nation of Israel as two of the most important conditions of the coming millennium. There are, however, signs that Dispensationalism is beginning to lose its grip on the evangelical church with the criticisms from Reformed theology weakening the general attachment to it. Great teaching centres for promoting Dispensationalism such as the large Dallas Seminary are now modifying their Dispensationalism though these traditional views are still widely held by many Christians.

Historic Premillennialism
Historic Premillennialism is to be clearly distinguished from Dispensational Premillennialism. Historic Premillennialism was common in the early church. Chiliasm, as it was called, was the view of many of the church fathers, for example, Justin Martyr and Irenaeus, but was rejected by Augustine and so generally lost favour and was not current in the Medieval church. At the Reformation, it was revived by many Anabaptists, but was rejected by Martin Luther, John Calvin and the other Reformers. Calvin described Chiliasm as 'too childish to refute'. In the early nineteenth century it was popularised again by Edward Irving in famous early morning lectures given at the Assembly time in Edinburgh in 1828. It was accepted by the brothers Andrew and Horatius Bonar, and by R. M. M'Cheyne. The famous London Baptist preacher, Charles Haddon Spurgeon was also a

Premillennialist, though it is not given much emphasis in his sermons or writings.

This Premillennialism taught that Christ could return any day and when He did it would be to reign physically for 1000 years in Jerusalem. Revelation 20 is understood to teach that after a period of falling away and persecution, Christ will come physically to this world and raise Christians from the dead, the first resurrection, and they will reign with Christ for this 1000 years. The thousand years will be a period of peace and prosperity and gospel blessing when the promises of the Old Testament will be fulfilled and men will beat their swords into ploughshares and their spears into pruning hooks. This millennium will end with a little season of Satan's rebellion which will be put down by Christ. Then there will be the second resurrection when the wicked will be raised, judged, and the final state will begin.

Dispensational Premillennialism

Dispensational Premillennialism is, however, of much more recent origin. It has only been around for less than the last two hundred years; but during that time it has become so prominent that many thought one could not be an evangelical Christian unless he held to this position. It is much more elaborate, and goes much further than the older variety, and essentially is incompatible with Reformed theology and sound biblical exegesis. It is fanatically espoused by its adherents as a fundamental point of orthodoxy. Those who do not adhere to it are viewed as unbelieving liberals.

Dispensationalism was developed by J. N. Darby (1800-1892) who was one of the founders of the Plymouth Brethren. He was born in London of Anglo-Irish parents and began his education at Westminster School, London but completed it in Trinity College, Dublin, Ireland. He was ordained as an Anglican clergyman and began his ministry within the Church of Ireland. He saw some success in the conversion of Roman Catholics, but when the Archbishop required converts to swear allegiance to George IV as the rightful king of Ireland, this created antagonism amongst the Irish and so additions to the church ceased. Darby resigned in protest and over the next few years developed his distinctive theology. He began to believe that the 'kingdom' prophesied in Isaiah and the other Old Testament prophets, was entirely different from the Christian church. The basic idea is that Jesus Christ came to this world in order to be king ruling on the throne of David over the Jews in Jerusalem, but was rejected, so He turned to the Gentiles. One day, after the age of the church is over, he asserted, Christ will return to reign over the Jews. The Christian church among the Gentiles was a kind of after-thought and never meant to happen. Dispensationalism rejects Reformed theology and the idea that God is sovereign and has foreordained whatsoever comes to pass. Essentially Dispensationalists must be Arminian, believing in free will and that there is no fixed plan of God.

Dispensationalism considers all history as divided into dispensations, or economies of God, that is defined periods of time during which God dealt with man in different ways and in distinctive covenants each quite set apart from the others and the way of salvation changing according to the dispensation. Reformed theologians also talk about dispensations. They have the Old Testament dispensation of the covenant of grace as distinct from the New Testament. However, Reformed theologians view the way of salvation as essentially the same from the fall of man till the end of the world. Old Testament saints were saved by faith in the Christ who was to come and the work which He would do. Those in New Testament times are saved by looking back in faith to His coming and work. There are differences between the dispensations with blood sacrifices being offered in the Old Testament dispensation as types of Christ's sacrifice for us, but in essence there is only the one covenant of grace and all who are saved are saved by grace through faith in the finished work of Christ.

Dispensationalists go much further with their very different dispensations. Usually they distinguish seven such periods or dispensations: (1) Innocence (before the Fall), (2) Conscience (the Fall to Noah), (3) Human Government (Noah to Abraham), (4) Promise (Abraham to Moses), (5) Law (Moses to Christ), (6) Grace (the Church Age) and then (7) the Millennium. The Eternal State comes at the conclusion of this history of the world. The way to be saved is different in each dispensation. Each of these periods is a time during which man is tested in respect to obedience to some specific revelation of the will of God, and each time man fails. Man's failure leads to the replacement of the dispensation by a new one with a new test of obedience. In this way a new dispensation begins. The most important of these dispensations are the last three.

Errors of Dispensationalism

Dispensationalists draw a definite distinction between Israel and the Church. Traditional Dispensationalists teach that the Israelites of the Old Testament were saved by keeping the law. But this is clearly an error. Jesus made plain to Nicodemus who was under the old law dispensation that no one could be saved without being born again (John 3:3). Paul asserts that no one can be justified, pardoned, and accepted by God by keeping the law: 'Therefore by the deeds of the law there shall no flesh be justified in his sight: for by the law is the knowledge of sin' (Romans 3:20). In another epistle he writes, 'For by grace are ye saved through faith; and that not of yourselves: it is the gift of God: Not of works, lest any man should boast' (Ephesians 2:8-9). Salvation has always been by grace and always will be, in order that God will get all the glory and none can boast. The problem of so many Jews was this: 'For they being ignorant of God's righteousness, and going about to establish their own righteousness, have not submitted themselves unto the righteousness of God' (Romans 10:3). Neither Jews nor anyone else can get to Heaven by their good works, or by the keeping of the law or by the performing of ritual. Salvation is all of grace. It is made perfectly plain in Hebrews that the men and women in Old Testament times perished, not because they did not keep the law but because of unbelief: 'But with whom was he grieved forty years? was it not with them that had sinned, whose carcases fell in the wilderness? And to whom sware he that they should not enter into his rest, but to them that believed not? So we see that they could not enter in because of unbelief' (Hebrews 3:17-19).

DISPENSATIONAL PREMILLENNIALISM

The error of drawing a distinction between Israel and the church is shown when Stephen states concerning Moses: 'This is he, that was in the church in the wilderness with the angel which spake to him in the mount Sina, and with our fathers: who received the lively oracles to give unto us' (Acts 7:38). Here the word in the Greek for church is *ecclesia*, the common word used in the New Testament for the church. The Israelites who had left Egypt in the wilderness journey were God's church. The church is the people of God from the days of Adam till the present. There is essentially only one way of salvation. There are superficial differences but Israel was the church in Old Testament times. Outward membership of Israel was no more a guarantee of salvation than outward membership of the church today: 'For they are not all Israel, which are of Israel' (Romans 9:6).

Another error of the traditional Dispensationalists is to distinguish sharply the 'kingdom of heaven' as that which belongs to the church from the 'kingdom of God' as that which belongs to the Jews. A careful study of these terms will show that Matthew used the term 'kingdom of heaven' because he was largely writing with a Jewish audience in mind and the Jews preferred to use the term 'heaven' instead of using the holy name of 'God'. The same parables are used to explain what the kingdom of heaven is in Matthew and what the kingdom of God is in Mark and Luke.

Dispensationalists refer to the church as a 'parenthesis', a temporary interlude in the progress of Israel's history. They do not see the Church Period as prophesied in the Old Testament. They note that Paul wrote to the Colossians: 'I Paul am made a minister; who now rejoice in my sufferings for you, and fill up that which is behind of the afflictions of Christ in my flesh for his body's sake, which is the church: whereof I am made a minister, according to the dispensation of God which is given to me for you, to fulfil the word of God; even the mystery which hath been hid from ages and from generations, but now is made manifest to his saints: to whom God would make known what is the riches of the glory of this mystery among the Gentiles; which is Christ in you, the hope of glory' (Colossians 1:23-27).

A mystery in the New Testament is a secret, hidden in the past, but now revealed. Thus, the church composed of a few Jews and many Gentiles is something that was hidden in Old Testament times but is now disclosed. The Dispensationalists argue that the rejection of Christ by the Jews meant that God turned from them to the Gentiles, the Gospel was preached to them, many of them believed and were saved, and so we have the Church Dispensation.

This mystery is indeed the fact that salvation is not limited to the Jews but that the Gentiles also are saved. Though this was largely hidden in Old Testament times it was revealed in some of the prophets. James makes this clear at the Jerusalem council. When summing up he argues that the Gentiles do not have to keep the ceremonial law. He quotes Amos 9:11-12 in Acts 15:16-18: 'After this I will return, and will build again the tabernacle of David, which is fallen down; and I will build again the ruins thereof, and I will set it up: That the residue of men might seek after the Lord, and all the Gentiles, upon whom my name is called, saith the Lord, who doeth all these things'. He then argues, 'Known unto God are all his works from the beginning of the world'. God knew this in the days of Amos and indeed from the beginning of creation. God did not change his mind. It was always God's purpose to gather the Gentiles into His church.

Rapture!

We shall now turn from looking at Dispensationalism in general to considering its teaching regarding the future. Dispensationalist hermeneutics assert that the Bible and prophecy should, if at all possible, be interpreted literally, including numbers, periods of time and materials used in buildings. There is a tendency for Dispensationalists to fail to consider the whole context of a verse or chapter, to fail to note the different forms of literature in the Bible, and to fail to interpret the symbolic language as such. For example, from the latter chapters of Ezekiel they would argue that the temple will be rebuilt and sacrifices offered again. This is a denial of New Testament revelation and especially of the Epistle

DISPENSATIONAL PREMILLENNIALISM

to the Hebrews where Christ is presented as the last great sacrifice which did away with the need of any other.

Dispensationalists teach that Christ could come at any time. They lay great stress on what Paul writes to the Thessalonians: 'But I would not have you to be ignorant, brethren, concerning them which are asleep, that ye sorrow not, even as others which have no hope. For if we believe that Jesus died and rose again, even so them also which sleep in Jesus will God bring with him. For this we say unto you by the word of the Lord, that we which are alive and remain unto the coming of the Lord shall not prevent [precede] them which are asleep. For the Lord himself shall descend from heaven with a shout, with the voice of the archangel, and with the trump of God: and the dead in Christ shall rise first: Then we which are alive and remain shall be caught up together with them in the clouds, to meet the Lord in the air: and so shall we ever be with the Lord' (1 Thessalonians 4:13-17).

Dispensationalists teach that Christ will come first to snatch away or 'rapture' His people. When He appears, the saints who have died will arise and they will join those still alive, and meet the Lord in the air. From there they will disappear to Heaven where for seven years they will enjoy the wedding supper of the Lamb. There are many variations of this teaching but this would be the most common. They believe the first resurrection spoken of in Revelation 20:4-6 is the resurrection which they claim will take place before the rapture. Amillennialists and some Post-millennialists believe the first resurrection is the spiritual resurrection when someone is born again or regenerated. Other Post-millennialists believe the first resurrection is the great spiritual revival which takes place at the beginning of the millennium. Reformed theologians believe in only one physical resurrection at the end of the world. For Dispensationalists there are several resurrections, even more than just two.

We have noted that Dispensationalists speak of the church age as a parenthesis. So, when does it end? Obviously when the church saints are raptured to Heaven. Then God returns to His original plan with Israel and the Messiah. A distinction is drawn between Christ coming 'for His saints,' the Rapture, and Christ coming 'with His saints' at the end of the seven years. At the end of the seven-year period there will be another resurrection of the saints who died during that seven-year period.

Dispensationalists assert that during the time of the Great Tribulation on earth, which follows the Rapture there will be terrible persecution, Antichrist (the beast from the sea, Revelation 13) will be revealed, and He will reign on the earth. At that time the majority of Jews will be converted. Then Christ will return with his saints. Christ will land on the Mount of Olives which will cleave in two creating a new valley (Zechariah 14). The Christian Jews will flee into the new valley which is formed (Zechariah 14:5). Christ will fight against Antichrist in the battle of Armageddon and Antichrist will be destroyed. Satan will be bound and cast into the bottomless pit for the thousand years (Revelation 20).

Christ will now reign in Jerusalem with His believing Jews, over the whole earth for 1000 years. All nations will be subject to Him. The saints who have risen at the end of the seven-year tribulation along with the saints raptured at the beginning of that period will live and reign in Heaven for the thousand years. Two judgments will occur at this time, the judgment of the Gentiles who persecuted the people of God during the tribulation, and the judgment of the Jews (Ezekiel 20:33-38). Some dispensationalists distinguish seven different judgments and seven different resurrections.

The Millennium will be a time of great prosperity and peace. The promises in the prophetic passages of the Old Testament will be fulfilled. For example, the words of Isaiah: 'But with righteousness shall he judge the poor, and reprove with equity for the meek of the earth: and he shall smite the earth with the rod of his mouth, and with the breath of his lips shall he slay the wicked. And righteousness shall be the girdle of his loins, and faithfulness the girdle of his reins. The wolf also shall dwell with the lamb, and the leopard shall lie down with the kid; and the calf and the young lion and the fatling together; and a little child shall lead them. And the cow and the bear shall feed; their young ones shall lie down together: and the lion shall eat straw like the ox. And the sucking child shall play on the hole of the asp, and the weaned child shall put his hand on the cockatrice' den. They shall not hurt nor destroy in all my holy mountain: for the earth shall be full of the knowledge of the Lord, as the waters cover the sea' (Isaiah 11:4-9). The wolf shall literally dwell with the lamb and the lion shall literally eat straw like an ox.

In interpreting the final chapters of Ezekiel 40-48 it is argued that the temple in Jerusalem will be rebuilt and that sacrifices will be offered once more. But this seriously undermines the work of Christ. Old Testament priests offered sacrifices: 'Who serve unto the example and shadow of heavenly things' (Hebrews 8:5). 'But Christ being come an high priest of good things to come, by a greater and more perfect tabernacle, not made with hands, that is to say, not of this building; Neither by the blood of goats and calves, but by his own blood he entered in once into the holy place, having obtained eternal redemption for us. For if the blood of bulls and of goats, and the ashes of an heifer sprinkling the unclean, sanctifieth to the purifying of the flesh: How much more shall the blood of Christ, who through the eternal Spirit offered himself without spot to God, purge your conscience from dead works to serve the living God?' (Hebrews 9:11-14). 'So Christ was once offered to bear the sins of many; and unto them that look for him shall he appear the second time without sin unto salvation' (Hebrews 9:28). This is further proved in the following chapter: 'But this man, after he had offered one sacrifice for sins for ever, sat down on the right hand of God; from henceforth expecting till his enemies be made his footstool. For by one offering he hath perfected for ever them that are sanctified' (Hebrews 10:12-14). Christ's sacrifice of Himself made an end of all animal sacrifices. These types have been replaced: 'For it is not possible that the blood of bulls and of goats should take away sins' (Hebrews 10:4). Animal sacrifices have forever been replaced by the one sacrifice of Christ. Jesus said, 'Destroy this temple, and in three days I will raise it up. Then said the Jews, Forty and six years was this temple in building, and wilt thou rear it up in three days? But he spake of the temple of his body' (John 2:19-21). The earthly temple was destroyed by the Jews when they crucified Christ, but He has now built a better one which is His body, the church. The shadows are gone and we now have the reality. There can be no return to these shadows.

Following this glorious millennium, Dispensationalists believe Satan will be loosed for a little while. He will gather nominal Christians and unbelievers and rebel with a great army against Christ, but he will be crushed by Christ. Then the resurrection of the saints who died during the Millennium will take place and the second resurrection of all unbelievers takes place, in contrast with the first resurrection of Revelation 20:5. The final judgment of the great white throne will follow and then the eternal state. The Jews will have their eternal state in the new earth, but the church, composed of Christian Jews and Gentiles will have their eternal state in Heaven. Many modern Dispensationalists have moved from these extremes and see only one final state for all the people of God, but this is the traditional Dispensational view.

There is a real problem for all Premillennialists. It is that Christ is already on the throne and reigning over Heaven and earth. Peter at Pentecost proclaimed that God raised up Christ from the dead and placed Him on the throne over all: 'Therefore being by the right hand of God exalted, and having received of the Father the promise of the Holy Ghost, he hath shed forth this, which ye now see and hear. For David is not ascended into the heavens: but he saith himself, The Lord said unto my Lord, Sit thou on my right hand, Until I make thy foes thy footstool. Therefore let all the house of Israel know assuredly, that God hath made the same Jesus, whom ye have crucified, both Lord and Christ' (Acts 2:33-36). Christ's ascension was immediately followed by His coronation. This reigning of Christ in His kingdom of power which has already begun, is spoken of by Paul as a kingdom which at the end of the world will be handed over to the Father: 'Then cometh the end, when he shall have delivered up the kingdom to God, even the Father; when he shall have put down all rule and all authority and power. For he must reign, till he hath put all enemies under his feet. The last enemy that shall be destroyed is death' (1 Corinthians 15:24-26).

DISPENSATIONAL PREMILLENNIALISM

Paul similarly refers to Christ's coronation as immediately following His resurrection and ascension when he writes to the Philippians: 'And being found in fashion as a man, he humbled himself, and became obedient unto death, even the death of the cross. Wherefore God also hath highly exalted him, and given him a name which is above every name: That at the name of Jesus every knee should bow, of things in heaven, and things in earth, and things under the earth; And that every tongue should confess that Jesus Christ is Lord, to the glory of God the Father' (Philippians 2:8-11).

For the Christ who is already reigning over all angels and men in the beautiful, sinless perfection of Heaven to return to this world to reign over the Jews in a sinful world would be a second humiliation. Surely Christ's sufferings are over! How could Christ return to this world when He in His humiliation exclaimed, 'O faithless and perverse generation, how long shall I be with you? how long shall I suffer you?' (Matthew 17:17)? It was painful for Christ to live among sinners. But now Christ's humiliation is over and His exaltation has begun. He will never again fight hand to hand with the devil. He crushed his head at Calvary. He came the first time that, 'through death he might destroy him that had the power of death, that is, the devil' (Hebrews 2:14) and He succeeded. Praise His name!

Critical to Rapture-thinking are the words, 'Then we which are alive and remain shall be caught up together with them in the clouds, to meet the Lord in the air: and so shall we ever be with the Lord' (1 Thessalonians 4:17). There seems to be here the idea of Christians being caught up into the air. But it is important to notice the second half of the verse, 'so shall we ever be with the Lord.' Surely this is describing a permanent state. We will forevermore be at home with the Lord. The meeting will be in the air but this is simply the beginning of eternity. But what then is referred to by the words, 'them also which sleep in Jesus will God bring with him' (v14)? It refers simply to the souls of Christians who have died returning with Christ from Heaven at His second coming to be reunited with their bodies. The resurrection takes place immediately Christ returns.

The idea of multiple physical resurrections and multiple judgment days finds no support in the parables of Jesus. There is only one day of reckoning for all. The dragnet captures good and bad fish, and at the end of the world they are separated one from another (Matthew 13:47-50). The wheat is separated from the tares at the end of the world (Matthew 13:29-30). When Christ returns it will be to judge all. The righteous, or the sheep, will be placed on His right hand and the goats, or wicked, on His left (Matthew 25:32). Dispensational Premillennialism errs in building a whole system on a very narrow base. One or two verses are pushed to extremes. There is a failure to appreciate the symbolic language of many passages of the Scriptures especially when dealing with prophecy.

CHAPTER 7

THE SECOND COMING AND RESURRECTION

We have in past chapters looked at some of the events which must precede the second coming of Christ. For example, we believe that the Jews as a people, must first be converted to believe in Jesus as the Messiah. This in turn will lead to world-wide blessing upon the church. Others argue that Christ could come anytime. We must be careful not to be too dogmatic. As we noted before prophecy is notoriously difficult to interpret. When Christ came the first time most people were wrong in their expectations.

When will Christ return? No one knows. Those who have tried to predict it have been proved wrong time and again. Even Jesus, when on earth, did not know when He would return. Obviously as God He knows everything, but as a man He is limited. He said: 'But of that day and hour knoweth no man, no, not the angels of heaven, but my Father only' (Matthew 24:36). In these words He demonstrates the reality of His manhood.

His second coming will be sudden and unexpected by most, so Jesus warned: 'Therefore be ye also ready: for in such an hour as ye think not the Son of man cometh' (Matthew 24:44). There will certainly be dark days just before the end, because Jesus said, 'Then shall they deliver you up to be afflicted, and shall kill you: and ye shall be hated of all nations for my name's sake. And then shall many be offended, and shall betray one another, and shall hate one another. And many false prophets shall rise, and shall deceive many. And because iniquity shall abound, the love of many shall wax cold' (Matthew 24:9-12). Our Lord implied that there will be a great decline in Christianity when He said, 'Nevertheless when the Son of man cometh, shall he find faith on the earth?' (Luke 18:8). Will there be any faithful disciples left?

THE GLORIOUS FUTURE

Satan Loosed

Following the blessing of the Millennium we are told in Revelation: 'And when the thousand years are expired, Satan shall be loosed out of his prison, and shall go out to deceive the nations which are in the four quarters of the earth, Gog and Magog, to gather them together to battle: the number of whom is as the sand of the sea. And they went up on the breadth of the earth, and compassed the camp of the saints about, and the beloved city: and fire came down from God out of heaven, and devoured them. And the devil that deceived them was cast into the lake of fire and brimstone, where the beast and the false prophet are, and shall be tormented day and night for ever and ever' (Revelation 20:7-10). This speaks of a final apostasy and of great persecution just before Christ returns. After the blessing of the Millennium there will be a falling away. Satan will gather nominal Christians and unbelievers and make a final attempt to destroy the true church. The camp of the saints will be surrounded and the church threatened with extermination. But then the Lord will act and fire will come from Heaven and destroy Satan's forces. Then will be the final judgment and Satan himself will be cast into the lake of fire to be tormented forever.

This loosing of Satan just before the end is interesting. It creates a problem for those who follow the Amillennialist interpretation. The common belief today among Reformed Christians is that the thousand years begins at Calvary. There Christ by His great historical redemptive act on the cross, wrestled with Satan and crushed his head, while in the process Christ's own heel was crushed. Jesus explained that the strong man had to be bound before his goods could be spoiled or robbed. In a very real sense, Jesus did bind Satan the strong man so that his goods could be plundered (Mark 3:27). If that is what is meant by the binding of the dragon in Revelation 20, what is this 'loosing'? This is the weak point of the Amillennialist argument. Surely the work on the cross cannot be undone? The great redemptive act of Calvary was a once-for-all-time defeat of Satan. His head was crushed and it cannot be healed. So, in agreement with most of the Puritans and classic divines, we understand the Millennium as a period of blessing during the New Testament age and it is followed by a time of falling away.

A Glorious Appearing

Christ's return will be clear and obvious to all. None will doubt what is happening: 'For the Lord himself shall descend from heaven with a shout, with the voice of the archangel, and with the trump of God: and the dead in Christ shall rise first: then we which are alive and remain shall be caught up together with them in the clouds, to meet the Lord in the air: and so shall we ever be with the Lord' (1 Thessalonians 4:16-17). There will be a great shout which will be heard all over the world and indeed the universe, and that voice will raise the dead. The trumpet of God will sound and what a trumpet blast it will be! The second coming of Christ will not be announced on radio, television or social media. There will be no time for that. Jesus explained: 'Wherefore if they shall say unto you, Behold, he is in the desert; go not forth: behold, he is in the secret chambers; believe it not. For as the lightning cometh out of the east, and shineth even unto the west; so shall also the coming of the Son of man be' (Matthew 24:26-27). It will be sudden, largely unexpected, and witnessed by all who are alive.

When Christ returns, He will bring with him the souls of His people who have been enjoying Paradise with Him: 'Them also which sleep in Jesus will God bring with him' (1 Thessalonians 4:14). These returning souls will immediately enter into the bodies which they left behind at death. Their bodies will be reconstituted by the miraculous, creative power of God and arise when the soul returns into them. The Thessalonians thought that those saints who had died would miss out on the return and appearing of Christ in glory, but no. Paul assured them and us that before anything else happens, 'the dead in Christ shall rise first' (v16). So, before the transformation of the living, the graves will opened and the dead arise. Then those still alive will be changed and, along with those who have been resurrected, they will meet Christ in the air and forevermore be with the Lord.

THE GLORIOUS FUTURE

Resurrection – 1 Corinthians 15

The portion of Scripture which particularly deals with the resurrection is 1 Corinthians 15. This chapter begins with Paul describing the gospel which he preached and which the Corinthians had received and by which they were saved. Central to that gospel is the vital truth of the resurrection of Christ which was witnessed by many different people. But there were teachers in Corinth who were saying that there will be no resurrection. The whole idea of the resurrection of the body was ridiculed by the Greek philosophers. When Paul mentioned the resurrection in his sermon on Mars Hill in Athens it brought an end to his sermon, 'some mocked: and others said, We will hear thee again of this matter' (Acts 17:32).

Paul, here, in writing to the Corinthians argues that if there is no resurrection, then Christ is not risen. And if Christ be not risen Paul's preaching was false, because the resurrection was central to his preaching. He said to the Romans that the Lord Jesus Christ, 'was delivered for our offences, and was raised again for our justification' (Romans 4:25). But more than that Paul is telling the Corinthians that their faith was useless, 'your faith is also vain' (1 Corinthians 15:14), if there is no resurrection. It would imply that Paul himself was a false witness. Further, it would imply that the Corinthians were still in their sins and those who have died believing in Jesus have perished (v18). Without the resurrection our Saviour is dead and a dead Saviour cannot save us. He could not even save Himself. Paul proceeds with his powerful reasoning, 'If in this life only we have hope in Christ, we are of all men most miserable' (v19). When the Apostle reflects on all he has suffered to communicate the Gospel – the beatings, whippings, imprisonments, shipwrecks, hunger, thirst, cold, heat, weariness – what was the point of it? All his many labours were for a lie. Surely the Corinthians will not believe that and neither will we!

So Paul proceeds to assert that Christ has actually risen and He is the first-fruits of those who died as believers and in that sense fell asleep. Since Jesus, the first-fruits, has arisen, those who sleep in Jesus will rise too. By man came death, that is through Adam and his first sin, so also by man, that is Christ, the last Adam, comes the resurrection. Christ rose first and so those who are in Christ will arise too.

Then comes the end when Christ delivers up His kingdom of power to the Father (v24). This is the kingdom He was given when He ascended after His resurrection. He was made head over all things for the benefit of His church (Ephesians 1:22). He said to His disciples, in anticipation of His coronation, 'All power is given unto me in heaven and in earth' (Matthew 28:18). Paul asserts, 'For he must reign, till he hath put all enemies under his feet' (1 Corinthians 15:25). Then He hands over this kingdom of power to His Father. There are no more enemies to be fought and overcome. His success is complete. But He still, of course, remains King and Head of His people.

We are told that, 'The last enemy that shall be destroyed is death' (1 Corinthians 15:26). Christ in His personal resurrection conquered death and at the end of the world He will conquer death in raising His people from the dead. Christ having Himself conquered all and risen victorious over death, He has also conquered death for His people and merited their resurrection so that they too will no longer be held under the power of death.

Paul challenges the Corinthians by reminding them what he suffered to bring the gospel to them. Why would he put himself in constant danger of hardship and of persecution? What was the point of him fighting with beasts at Ephesus if the dead rise not? It would seem more sensible to change one's philosophy and live for the pleasures of the moment: 'Let us eat and drink; for tomorrow we die' (v32). But then he warns, 'Be not deceived'. Evil companions will lead astray. Beware of learning from those around you, rather than learning from the Lord!

What is the Resurrection Body Like?

The question is sometimes asked: What sort of body will the resurrected individuals have? There are different kinds of flesh and different kinds of bodies around. There is the flesh of men, of animals, of birds and of fish. There are earthly bodies and heavenly bodies and each has its own glory. Paul explains that there will be an identity between the present body and the resurrection body and yet there will be differences. When a seed is placed in the ground and grows, a plant appears. There is an identity between the seed and the plant and yet there are great differences. It is the same body that is planted in the grave and that which arises in the resurrection and yet it is different: 'It is sown in corruption; it is raised in incorruption: it is sown in dishonour; it is raised in glory: it is sown in weakness; it is raised in power: it is sown a natural body; it is raised a spiritual body. There is a natural body, and there is a spiritual body. And so it is written, The first man Adam was made a living soul; the last Adam was made a quickening spirit. Howbeit that was not first which is spiritual, but that which is natural; and afterward that which is spiritual' (1 Corinthians 15:42-46). The body of the Christian which rises from the grave will be fit for eternity in Heaven. In this life our bodies are subject to ageing, disease, death and decay, but the resurrection body will be glorious, powerful, spiritual and eternal. It will neither hunger nor thirst. It will not need sleep as there is no night there. Christ was able to pass through closed doors in His resurrection body, to move quickly from one place to another and was not constantly subject to gravity. It is possible that the resurrected saints will be similar. They will be able to meet Christ in the air when He returns.

At the point of Christ's return the dead Christians will rise first and then those saints who are alive will be transformed and given similar resurrection bodies: 'We shall not all sleep, but we shall all be changed, in a moment, in the twinkling of an eye, at the last trump: for the trumpet shall sound, and the dead shall be raised incorruptible, and we shall be changed. For this corruptible must put on incorruption, and this mortal must put on immortality. So when this corruptible shall have put on incorruption, and this mortal shall have put on immortality, then shall be brought to pass the saying that is written, Death is swallowed up in victory' (vv51-54). At this point death is forever conquered for the believer and all the effects of the curse are removed. The law said that sin must be punished with death and the sinner return to the ground out of which he was taken, 'Dust thou art, and unto dust shalt thou return' (Genesis 3:19). But through the work of Christ, at the resurrection, God's people will be able to say, 'O death, where is thy sting? O grave, where is thy victory? The sting of death is sin; and the strength of sin is the law. But thanks be to God, which giveth us the victory through our Lord Jesus Christ' (1 Corinthians 15:55-57). We see the godly dying as the snake of death stings them, because we are all sinners. Without sin there would be no death. But one day the full effects of the atonement will be seen as Christ removes the sting from the snake. We have witnessed the grave devouring all our Christian friends. It seems completely victorious, but one day we will be able to look the grave in the face and say, 'Where is your victory now?'

Do the wicked rise too?
What happens to the ungodly when Christ returns? It will be a terrifying time for the wicked. Their false religion will be shown up for what it is. The atheists will be exposed as fools. God reveals Himself in creation and has left a witness to Himself in every conscience so that it is the fool that says in his heart that there is no God (Psalm 14:1). O the fear that will be everywhere when the final trumpet sounds! 'And the kings of the earth, and the great men, and the rich men, and the chief captains, and the mighty men, and every bondman, and every free man, hid themselves in the dens and in the rocks of the mountains; And said to the mountains and rocks, Fall on us, and hide us from the face of him that sitteth on the throne, and from the wrath of the Lamb: for the great day of his wrath is come; and who shall be able to stand?' (Revelation 6:15-19). Many who never prayed before will now pray, but it is too late. They will know now for sure that they will receive according to their deeds and that there is no escape. They are all sinners and there is no hiding place. Their conscience will condemn them and every mouth shall be stopped.

Some have argued that only the godly who are entitled to eternal life will rise from the dead. However, Scripture makes plain that the resurrection will be general. It is stated that good and bad will rise from the graves. Daniel's prophecy reveals this: 'And many of them that sleep in the dust of the earth shall awake, some to everlasting life, and some to shame and everlasting contempt' (Daniel 12:2). 'Many' here does not mean that some will not arise but rather that the numbers who will arise will be very many. Our Lord when on earth also declared that there would be a general resurrection: 'Marvel not at this: for the hour is coming, in the which all that are in the graves shall hear his voice, and shall come forth; they that have done good, unto the resurrection of life; and they that have done evil, unto the resurrection of damnation' (John 5:28-29). The same truth is revealed in the Book of Revelation: 'And the sea gave up the dead which were in it; and death and hell delivered up the dead which were in them: and they were judged every man according to their works' (Revelation 20:13).

The wicked will have bodies that cannot die but yet will be always dying. Immediately the unconverted die they go to Hell in their souls and so in a conscious state they begin to suffer there. At the end of the world they will return in their souls to enter into their bodies. All the bodies of the ungodly will be resurrected just like the godly. There will however be one vital difference. The bodies of true Christians are redeemed and will fully reflect the image of God (Romans 8:23). The new bodies of the unconverted will be in the image of the devil, suited for suffering in Hell forever. Eternity in Hell, what a thought! The resurrected ungodly shall feel pain in their new bodies as well as in their souls. At present in Hell they are suffering only in their souls, but with their resurrected bodies they will suffer even more: 'And the smoke of their torment ascendeth up for ever and ever' (Revelation 14:11).

Treatment of dead bodies

It is important to remember that the bodies of believers are precious and should be treated with great respect. In regeneration, or the new birth, we are united to, and planted in Christ. We are all composed of a body and a soul and it is as such that we are united to Christ. Both our body and soul are united to Christ, so even the dead body of the believer is mysteriously united to the Lord. The *Westminster Larger Catechism* gives a wonderful answer to Question 86: 'What is the communion in glory with Christ, which the members of the invisible church enjoy immediately after death?'

THE SECOND COMING AND RESURRECTION

Answer: 'The communion in glory with Christ, which the members of the invisible church enjoy immediately after death is, in that their souls are then made perfect in holiness, and received into the highest heavens, where they behold the face of God in light and glory, waiting for the full redemption of their bodies, which even in death continue united to Christ, and rest in their graves as in their beds, till at the last day they be again united to their souls. Whereas the souls of the wicked are at their death cast into hell, where they remain in torments and utter darkness, and their bodies kept in their graves, as in their prisons, till the resurrection and judgment of the great day'.

These are great truths drawn from the Scripture. The body of a believer is precious being still united to Christ. It rests in the grave as in a bed. Therefore, the mutilation of bodies is wicked. It appears most Scriptural and godly to follow the example of the saints of old and so to bury the bodies of our loved ones rather than to cremate them. The common modern practice of cremation arose from those who were atheists and thought that by burning the body they could so destroy it, that there could be no resurrection for them on day of judgment. However, it does not matter what happens to the body after death, God will raise it. Even if it is burnt to ashes and scattered by wind and waves to the four corners of the earth, God will cause it to arise. Even if it is sent into distant space, God the Almighty will gather it up, bring it back, resurrect the individual and judge him. Suppose cannibals ate the body and other cannibals ate these cannibals, God the all-powerful Creator will ensure that the individual is raised and that the body's identity will continue. It is worth remembering that almost all of the cells in our own bodies are changed over our lifetime, yet our identity remains. Christ left no part of His body behind in the grave. All was transformed into His resurrection body.

Perfect bodies

When we rise from the dead our body will be perfect and like that of Christ. Paul wrote to the Philippians: 'For our conversation is in heaven; from whence also we look for the Saviour, the Lord Jesus Christ: who shall change our vile body, that it may be fashioned like unto his glorious body, according to the working whereby he is able even to subdue all things unto himself' (Philippians 3:20-21). Our body today is a humble body, a body that belongs to our state of humiliation, but one day we will have a glorified body. Further our body will be transformed to be like that of Christ. God is able to do this and has assured us it will happen.

What about those with deformed bodies in this world? Deformed bodies are the result of the Fall and in Heaven all the results of the Fall and sin will be removed. Every body in glory will be perfect.

What about those who die as infants? They too will have perfect, normal, mature human bodies. The same is true even for children lost by miscarriage or killed by abortion. Once the child is conceived in the womb, God creates a soul which unites with the fetus and a separate human being is made. Elect infants who die in the womb will be part of the heavenly family of God around the throne, but they will be there as adults. For all we know, all such infants who die in the womb or who die as infants, are elect.

Marriage in Heaven?

Jesus was asked by the Sadducees about marriage in Heaven. They did not believe in the resurrection and tried to catch out our Lord by asking about a woman who successively had had seven husbands and then died childless. Who would be her husband in Heaven? Jesus replied: 'Ye do err, not knowing the scriptures, nor the power of God. For in the resurrection they neither marry, nor are given in marriage, but are as the angels of God in heaven' (Matthew 22:29-30). So, there will be no marriage in Heaven or special relationships of that kind. But will there be male or female? We see no reason why not.

Sometimes it is asked whether we will know one another in Heaven? If we know one another on earth, then why not in Heaven? We will not be more ignorant there. Peter, James, and John seemed immediately able to recognise Moses and Elijah on the Mount of Transfiguration. The disciples had difficulty recognising Jesus after His resurrection but that seemed to be because in their unbelief they did not expect Him to be risen. Also, we are told on at least one occasion that God withheld their vision, 'But their eyes were holden that they should not know him' (Luke 24:16).

Transformation of the World
It is not simply men and women who will experience transformation when Christ returns. The universe will also be as it were born again. Paul describes the whole creation as under the curse of God and longing for the regeneration which will involve the formation of the new heavens and new earth: 'For the earnest expectation of the creature waiteth for the manifestation of the sons of God. For the creature was made subject to vanity, not willingly, but by reason of him who hath subjected the same in hope, Because the creature itself also shall be delivered from the bondage of corruption into the glorious liberty of the children of God. For we know that the whole creation groaneth and travaileth in pain together until now. And not only they, but ourselves also, which have the firstfruits of the Spirit, even we ourselves groan within ourselves, waiting for the adoption, to wit, the redemption of our body' (Romans 8:19-23). The creation as it came from the hand of God in the beginning was very good and is described as such by God Himself. However when man sinned even the inanimate creation was affected: 'Cursed is the ground for thy sake; in sorrow shalt thou eat of it all the days of thy life; thorns also and thistles shall it bring forth to thee; and thou shalt eat the herb of the field; in the sweat of thy face shalt thou eat bread, till thou return unto the ground; for out of it wast thou taken: for dust thou art, and unto dust shalt thou return' (Genesis 3:17-19). Thorns and thistles, weeds and nettles were produced. Also, disease and death affected all life. Further, even the physical world was affected with storms, tornadoes, earthquakes and volcanoes. These things show the creation writhing in agony waiting for the day of deliverance when Christ will come again and restore the creation. The whole creation is waiting for the revelation of the children of God.

It is interesting to notice the term used here to describe the end point of adoption, 'the redemption of our body' (Romans 8:23). The redemptive work of Christ is not completed until the body is redeemed as well as the soul. All the disfiguration of sin will be gone and our bodies will be like Christ's glorified body. Then, and only then, will we be fully renewed in the image of God, body as well as soul. The image of God will shine through our body.

Peter speaks about the change which will take place in the world. He answers the mockers who object and say why has Christ not returned yet. The years are passing and did He not say that He would come soon? Peter notes what it was like in the days of Noah. Then there were scoffers too. God gave to the ancient world a hundred and twenty years in which to repent: 'But, beloved, be not ignorant of this one thing, that one day is with the Lord as a thousand years, and a thousand years as one day. The Lord is not slack concerning his promise, as some men count slackness; but is longsuffering to us-ward, not willing that any should perish, but that all should come to repentance' (2 Peter 3:8-9). The Lord in His kindness gives people plenty of time to repent and prepare for His return. But then one day, suddenly, He will come and Peter describes what it will be like: 'But the day of the Lord will come as a thief in the night; in the which the heavens shall pass away with a great noise, and the elements shall melt with fervent heat, the earth also and the works that are therein shall be burned up. Seeing then that all these things shall be dissolved, what manner of persons ought ye to be in all holy conversation and godliness, looking for and hasting unto the coming of the day of God, wherein the heavens being on fire shall be dissolved, and the elements shall melt with fervent heat? Nevertheless we, according to his promise, look for new heavens and a new earth, wherein dwelleth righteousness' (2 Peter 3:10-13).

The world will end with the coming of Christ. The heavens will be rolled up like a scroll and pass out of existence (Revelation 6:14). This earth will be consumed with fire and out of the conflagration will come the new heavens and the new earth. Then will be the final judgment and the eternal state.

CHAPTER 8

THE JUDGMENT

Following the resurrection comes the final judgment. Historical Premillennialists and Dispensationalists have several resurrections and several judgments. Dispensationalists have a judgment of saints at the rapture and then, seven years later when Jesus returns again, a judgment of the Jews converted during the seven year period of the tribulation, and then also the judgment of the nations which they see as separate. Finally the judgment from the great white throne on the last day, following the Millennium. The Bible however describes only one judgment day which comes at the end of world history. True, when an individual dies immediately they go either to Heaven or Hell, but it is not a judgment and there is no appearing before a judge or examination of evidence. From the parable of the Rich Man and Lazarus it is plain that when the unconverted die they open their eyes in Hell (Luke 16:23). In contrast, the converted open their eyes in Heaven. The angels carried the soul of Lazarus to Abraham's bosom (v22). The penitent thief was assured, 'Today shalt thou be with me in paradise' (Luke 23:43). For the true Christian, to be absent from the body is to be present with the Lord (2 Corinthians 5:8). The Psalmist states, 'As for me, I will behold thy face in righteousness: I shall be satisfied, when I awake, with thy likeness' (Psalm 17:15).

An individual's destiny is fixed the moment he dies. John the Baptist warned, 'And now also the axe is laid unto the root of the trees: every tree therefore which bringeth not forth good fruit is hewn down, and cast into the fire' (Luke 3:9). In Ecclesiastes it is explained that as the tree falls so shall it lie: 'If the tree fall toward the south, or toward the north, in the place where the tree falleth, there it shall be' (Ecclesiastes 11:3).

THE GLORIOUS FUTURE

The purpose of the Judgment Day

What then is the purpose of the judgment day? It will change nothing. The destiny of each individual is already fixed. The purpose of the judgment day is to reveal God's justice and mercy. It will demonstrate the righteousness of the righteous and the wickedness of the wicked. God's people will be openly acknowledged and acquitted. The wickedness of the wicked will be fully exposed. All secrets of every heart and life will be revealed and, as it has been said, there will be a resurrection of the reputations of the righteous who have often been maligned in this world. Hypocrites will be unmasked. Every mouth shall be stopped and all mankind will acknowledge that God is just and right and true.

John received a revelation of what will happen at the end of the world. There will be a great falling away from the faith. Satan, being loosed, will gather his forces to persecute and destroy the Christian church. It will seem as if the Lord's people are about to be exterminated. The camp of God's people, the church, will be as it were surrounded, but then fire comes down from Heaven and burns up their enemies. Satan is arrested and cast into the lake of fire to be tormented day and night for ever and ever. The end of the world has come.

The Last Day

The judgment day has arrived: 'And I saw a great white throne, and him that sat on it, from whose face the earth and the heaven fled away; and there was found no place for them. And I saw the dead, small and great, stand before God; and the books were opened: and another book was opened, which is the book of life: and the dead were judged out of those things which were written in the books, according to their works. And the sea gave up the dead which were in it; and death and hell delivered up the dead which were in them: and they were judged every man according to their works. And death and hell were cast into the lake of fire. This is the second death. And whosoever was not found written in the book of life was cast into the lake of fire' (Revelation 20:11-15).

THE JUDGMENT

We notice here that a great white throne is set up. It is a great throne because it is vastly above every other throne, and before this throne all will have to give account. It is the judgment throne of God, the supreme Being. It is white. Let none worry that he or she will not receive justice. This throne is pure and the justice administered will be perfect. No bribery or corruption will take place. No preferential treatment will be offered to any. God is no respecter of persons (Acts 10:34).

Who will judge the world?

Who sits on the throne? It is the One 'from whose face the earth and the heaven fled away; and there was found no place for them' (Revelation 20:11). Paul explains further that God, 'hath appointed a day, in the which he will judge the world in righteousness by that man whom he hath ordained; whereof he hath given assurance unto all men, in that he hath raised him from the dead' (Acts 17:31). Christ humbled Himself to death for the salvation of His people and then God exalted Him by His resurrection, His ascension, His sitting at the right hand of God and then His coming to judge the world at the last day.

In the British justice system juries composed of fellow-citizens are employed, so that the individual is judged by his peers. God will judge us by a man, again one of ourselves, and One who 'was in all points tempted like as we are, yet without sin' (Hebrews 4:15). Jesus fully understands what it is like to live in this world, constantly tempted by sin and Satan. None will be able to turn to the Judge and say you do not know how hard it was to live in this world. Our Lord stated: 'For the Father judgeth no man, but hath committed all judgment unto the Son: That all men should honour the Son, even as they honour the Father. He that honoureth not the Son honoureth not the Father which hath sent him' (John 5:22-23). It is the God-man, the Saviour who died on the cross for our sins, who will be the Judge. That is a great encouragement to the Christian. Our Mediator, Friend and Brother is the Judge.

Who will be judged?

Who will be judged? John states, 'I saw the dead, small and great, stand before God' (Revelation 20:12). The kings and mighty men of the earth will be there, celebrities but also ordinary folk, working men and women, the destitute and primitive people. It does not matter what happens to the body. We are told, 'the sea gave up the dead which were in it; and death and hell delivered up the dead which were in them' (v13). Some are drowned at sea. Their bodies are eaten by crabs and other sea creatures. These creatures are eaten by others. But still the sea will give up those who died in it. Even if the body is burnt and the ashes scattered on the waters, the sea will give them up. Almighty God will raise them up. Death will deliver up all who died. Hades, the realm of the dead, and even the realm of the wicked dead, will send their dead to stand before the throne. Nebuchadnezzar and Cyrus, the Pharaohs and the Caesars, Stalin, and Hitler, they will all be there, along with the peasants, the slaves and the disabled. The great patriarchs, the prophets, the apostles, the martyrs, the reformers, along with ordinary Christian men and women will be judged. Boys and girls will all be there. Muslims, Hindus, Buddhists, and atheists will be there.

Some think Christians will not be judged but the Scripture is clear that all will be judged. Paul wrote: 'We shall all stand before the judgment seat of Christ. For it is written, As I live, saith the Lord, every knee shall bow to me, and every tongue shall confess to God. So then, every one of us shall give account of himself to God' (Romans 14:10-12). Paul includes himself and the Roman Christians among those judged. In another Epistle he further emphasised this when he wrote: 'For we must all appear before the judgment seat of Christ; that every one may receive the things done in his body, according to that he hath done, whether it be good or bad. Knowing therefore the terror of the Lord, we persuade men; but we are made manifest unto God; and I trust also are made manifest in your consciences' (2 Corinthians 5:10-11). Christians must also appear before God's judgment seat to give their account.

THE JUDGMENT

What is the standard used in judgment?

What is the standard used in judgment? We are told that the 'books were opened: and another book was opened, which is the book of life: and the dead were judged out of those things which were written in the books, according to their works' (Revelation 20:12). God partially reveals Himself and His will in nature and in the human conscience. Everyone has some knowledge of the law of God. Sadly, individuals do not even live up to that standard. God has given a much fuller revelation of His law and gospel in the Scriptures. The Bible teaches what man is to believe concerning God and what duty God requires of man. Judges on earth judge according to the law of the land and so the divine Judge judges according to the law of God. Sin is a crime against God and is defined as 'any lack of conformity unto, or transgression of, the law of God' (Westminster Shorter Catechism, Answer 14). The 'books' which are opened on the judgment day contain a complete record of our lives. Our lives are measured according to God's Word.

The Book of Life

We are also told here about a 'book of life'. It is important to remember that the language is symbolic. There is no actual book but it is as if there were, and the picture or metaphor of a book helps us to understand what is implied. It is as it were a register of those who will receive eternal life. This book is referred to several times in the Old Testament. In relation to the enemies of the Messiah the Psalmist states: 'Let them be blotted out of the book of the living, and not be written with the righteous' (Psalm 69:28). In another Psalm we find the words: 'Thine eyes did see my substance, yet being unperfect; and in thy book all my members were written' (Psalm 139:16). Daniel is told about a time of severe persecution and some would be preserved because their names were in the book: 'There shall be a time of trouble, such as never was since there was a nation even to that same time: and at that time thy people shall be delivered, every one that shall be found written in the book' (Daniel 12:1).

THE GLORIOUS FUTURE

In the New Testament there are seven references to this book in the Book of Revelation. The persevering faithful are encouraged by Christ, 'I will not blot out his name out of the book of life, but I will confess his name before my Father, and before his angels' (Revelation 3:5). Later we are told of the beast that arises out of the sea, 'And all that dwell upon the earth shall worship him, whose names are not written in the book of life of the Lamb slain from the foundation of the world' (Revelation 13:8). Here the book of life is equated with the elect. Later we read of those 'whose names were not written in the book of life from the foundation of the world' (Revelation 17:8). This makes plain that the names were entered into this book in eternity, before the creation of the world. None shall enter Heaven but those whose names are in the book of life (Revelation 21:27). A warning is given to those who remove or delete part of the Scriptures that, 'God shall take away his part out of the book of life, and out of the holy city, and from the things which are written in this book' (Revelation 22:19).

So, whose names are in the book of life? It is plain that it is the elect of God. But who are the elect? Only God knows. Another way of looking at the book of life is to think of it as all true Christians. John wrote, 'He that hath the Son hath life; and he that hath not the Son of God hath not life' (1 John 5:12). We possess the Son of God when we by faith receive and embrace Him as our own personal Saviour. He is freely offered to all. Those, however, who are dead in sin see nothing precious in Christ, hate Him and will not believe in Him. Those who are in the elect are effectually called, and regenerated by the Holy Spirit and convicted of their sin and their need of a Saviour and are granted the gift of faith to believe in Him. Eventually, all the elect will believe in Jesus in this life. Revelation 22 warns of some whose names will be removed from the book of life. Surely if the book contains the names of the elect this could never happen? But there are many who think their names are in the book of life. They show by their rejection of Scripture that they are not true believers and so in that sense their names are removed. Also, we have here a warning to the faithful. Paul warned the Corinthians, 'Wherefore let him that thinketh he standeth take

THE JUDGMENT

heed lest he fall' (1 Corinthians 10:12). There is a huge difference between thinking you stand and actually standing.

On the judgment day we could say that the first book considered is the book of life. All whose names are in the book of life will enter Heaven and all whose names are not in the book of life are cast into the lake of fire. So a radical distinction is drawn between the righteous and the wicked. There is no gradation between the two. There is no dubiety as to who gets to Heaven.

Justified by Works
Sometimes it is stated that we are justified by faith in this life but we will be justified by works on the day. There is a sense in which this is true. Paul wrote, 'Therefore being justified by faith, we have peace with God through our Lord Jesus Christ' (Romans 5:1). Our initial justification is by faith alone. It is totally on the basis of the work of Christ. He atoned for our sin and His merit is our righteousness. James then writes that we are justified by works because our works show the nature of our faith and whether it is real saving faith or not: 'Even so faith, if it hath not works, is dead, being alone. Yea, a man may say, Thou hast faith, and I have works: shew me thy faith without thy works, and I will shew thee my faith by my works' (James 2:17-18). He adds, 'Ye see then how that by works a man is justified, and not by faith only' (v24). He concludes, 'For as the body without the spirit is dead, so faith without works is dead also' (v26). Jesus said, 'By their fruits ye shall know them' (Matthew 7:20). In that sense we will be judged by our works on the judgment day, whether they be good or evil. Our works show that our faith is true saving faith.

The Judgment Day
Our Lord Jesus presents us with a vivid picture of the judgment day in Matthew's Gospel: 'When the Son of man shall come in his glory, and all the holy angels with him, then shall he sit upon the throne of his glory: And before him shall be gathered all nations: and he shall separate them one from another, as a shepherd divideth his sheep from the goats: And

he shall set the sheep on his right hand, but the goats on the left' (Matthew 25:31-33). When Christ returns it will be to judge, not to 'rapture' saints, nor to perform some preliminary judgment of the nations. Every man and woman will be brought before Him and He will separate them one from another as a shepherd does the sheep from the goats. One group will be set on His right hand and the other on His left. To those on His right hand He will say, 'Come, ye blessed of my Father, inherit the kingdom prepared for you from the foundation of the world' (v34). To them is given the new heavens and the new earth. To those on His left He will say: 'Depart from me, ye cursed, into everlasting fire, prepared for the devil and his angels' (v41). It is worth noticing that Hell was prepared initially for the devil and his angels and not for mankind. But sinners who do not believe in Jesus and reject the gospel will end up there. And then it is added, 'And these shall go away into everlasting punishment: but the righteous into life eternal' (v46). It is not some temporary judgment but a final one. The word used in the Greek for describing the state of the righteous and the wicked is the same, and should be translated 'eternal'. For the one they enter into eternal life and for the other into eternal misery.

The Basis for Judgment

The basis for the judgment is enlightening. He shall say to those on His right hand: 'For I was an hungred, and ye gave me meat: I was thirsty, and ye gave me drink: I was a stranger, and ye took me in: naked, and ye clothed me: I was sick, and ye visited me: I was in prison, and ye came unto me' (Matthew 25:35-36). Interestingly the godly feel that they have done nothing worthy of Heaven. 'Then shall the righteous answer him, saying, Lord, when saw we thee an hungred, and fed thee? or thirsty, and gave thee drink? When saw we thee a stranger, and took thee in? or naked, and clothed thee? Or when saw we thee sick, or in prison, and came unto thee?' (vv37-39). But the Judge responds, 'Verily I say unto you, Inasmuch as ye have done it unto one of the least of these my brethren, ye have done it unto me' (v40). Where true faith is, it cannot remain alone and it must express itself in works. These works demonstrate the reality of the faith.

THE JUDGMENT

Showing love to a Christian for Christ's sake shows that a man or woman has been born again. Love to Christ and His people is a great mark of the Christian.

Similarly, we see the judgment of the wicked. The King will say to those on His left hand: 'Depart from me, ye cursed, into everlasting fire, prepared for the devil and his angels: for I was an hungred, and ye gave me no meat: I was thirsty, and ye gave me no drink: I was a stranger, and ye took me not in: naked, and ye clothed me not: sick, and in prison, and ye visited me not' (vv41-43). But they are pictured as responding in surprise: 'Lord, when saw we thee an hungred, or athirst, or a stranger, or naked, or sick, or in prison, and did not minister unto thee?' (v44). Notice their self-righteousness. But the Judge explains, 'Verily I say unto you, Inasmuch as ye did it not to one of the least of these, ye did it not to me' (v45). As we saw, where real faith exists it will express itself in love. A lack of care for the suffering of God's children shows a lack of love for Christ. No work done in faith and love for Christ will go unrewarded. The smallest action of love and kindness shown to a child of God is appreciated, 'Whosoever shall give to drink unto one of these little ones a cup of cold water only in the name of a disciple, verily I say unto you, he shall in no wise lose his reward' (Matthew 10:42).

Some might think from this that their good works will balance out their evil works. Muslims have this idea of the balances and hope that their good works will eventually out-weigh their evil works. But this is contrary to the true Christian religion though many professing Christians also think that way. There are and always have been many hypocrites in the church. Jesus told a parable to explain the impossibility of us being saved by our good works. Think, He said, if you have a servant or slave working in a field and at the end of the day he comes home. You do not say to him to sit down while you prepare a meal for him. You do not thank your servant for doing what he was commanded to do and what was his duty to do. So Jesus concludes, 'So likewise ye, when ye shall have done all those things which are commanded you, say, We are unprofitable servants: we have done that which was our duty to do' (Luke 17:10). Our duty is to keep all the commandments, all the time. We are to be doing good works constantly. If we are to be judged according to our works none of us would get to Heaven. One sin is enough to condemn us to Hell. We can only be saved by trusting in Christ to save us. His good works are meritorious. His death atones for our sins. We have no merit but the imputed merit of Christ. Once we are saved, however, our works show that we are truly saved and these works are purified from all wrong motives and faults by the blood of Christ. In this way they are pleasing to God.

Rewards and Punishment

Will there be different degrees of punishment in Hell and on the other hand varying degrees of reward in Heaven? Jesus makes plain that that is the case. He states that there will be some in a worse Hell than others. 'Then began he to upbraid the cities wherein most of his mighty works were done, because they repented not: Woe unto thee, Chorazin! woe unto thee, Bethsaida! for if the mighty works, which were done in you, had been done in Tyre and Sidon, they would have repented long ago in sackcloth and ashes. But I say unto you, It shall be more tolerable for Tyre and Sidon at the day of judgment, than for you. And thou, Capernaum, which art exalted unto heaven, shalt be brought down to hell: for if the mighty works, which have been done in thee, had been done in Sodom, it would have remained until this day. But I say unto you, That it shall be more tolerable for the land of Sodom in the day of judgment, than for thee' (Matthew 11:20-24). Some have greater privileges. Those who lived in Chorazin and Bethsaida saw the miracles of Christ which were signs from Heaven which demonstrated that Jesus was the Messiah. The people of Capernaum had experienced what it was for Jesus to live among them. These people of Galilee had heard wonderful teaching and seen His holy life. Jesus is saying that heathen who lived in cities like Tyre and Sidon would get off much lighter on the day of judgment than these privileged people. Sodom is set out in Scripture as the most wicked city because of its immorality, yet Jesus argues that if it had witnessed the teaching and miracles of Christ it would have repented. From this we can gather that there will be different degrees of punishment in Hell. The greater our privileges, and the more we know of the law and the gospel, and the more we witness around us of true Christianity, the greater our punishment and sufferings will be in Hell if we end up there.

One of the parables would seem to teach that the rewards of the righteous are the same no matter how long and diligently they labour for God. Jesus spoke of the owner of a vineyard who hired some men to work for a penny a day which was then the going rate. Later that day he went out and found other labourers unemployed and told them also to go and work in the vineyard and he would give them what was appropriate. In the late afternoon he found more unemployed workers and also sent them into the vineyard promising to pay them. At the end of the day the labourers were called and given their wages starting with those who worked only for one hour. He gave each of them a penny. When those who had worked all day came they thought they would be given more, but also received a penny. They then complained, 'These last have wrought but one hour, and thou hast made them equal unto us, which have borne the burden and heat of the day' (Matthew 20:12). But the owner rightly answered one of them, 'Friend, I do thee no wrong: didst not thou agree with me for a penny? Take that thine is, and go thy way: I will give unto this last, even as unto thee. Is it not lawful for me to do what I will with mine own? Is thine eye evil, because I am good? So the last shall be first, and the first last: for many be called, but few chosen' (Matthew 20:13-16). This parable is simply emphasising that salvation is by grace and none of us has any merit. We cannot demand anything. We all who trust in Jesus as our Saviour and follow Him will be welcomed into Heaven. Some have only laboured a short time but yet they too will enjoy a full Heaven. The penitent thief who was saved as he died on the cross beside Jesus will receive the same Heaven as the Apostle Paul, or a missionary who laboured all his life for the Master.

However, there are some other parables which teach that although all believers enter Heaven there will be differences of reward there. The parable of the talents (Matthew 25:14-30) and the parable of the pounds (Luke 19:11-27) both indicate that the rewards will vary. Further we are commanded by Christ 'But lay up for yourselves treasures in heaven, where neither moth nor rust doth corrupt, and where thieves do not break through nor steal' (Matthew 6:20). Wealth should be accumulated in the bank of Heaven rather than in earthly banks. Zeal and godliness are noted by God. Humble, faithful labour for Christ is rewarded. In the parable of the Unjust Steward, our Lord concludes: 'Make to yourselves friends of the mammon of unrighteousness; that, when ye fail, they may receive you into everlasting habitations' (Luke 16:9). There is a specially blessed Heaven for charitable Christians. All who have saving faith in Christ get Heaven but some will have a greater Heaven than others. All will be full but some will have a greater capacity to enjoy Heaven. Shells on the shore vary in size but when the tide comes in they are all full of water.

Paul wrote interesting words to the Corinthians: 'For other foundation can no man lay than that is laid, which is Jesus Christ. Now if any man build upon this foundation gold, silver, precious stones, wood, hay, stubble; every man's work shall be made manifest: for the day shall declare it, because it shall be revealed by fire; and the fire shall try every man's work of what sort it is. If any man's work abide which he hath built thereupon, he shall receive a reward. If any man's work shall be burned, he shall suffer loss: but he himself shall be saved; yet so as by fire' (1 Corinthians 3:11-15). It is made clear that on the judgment day some will be saved but their work lost. If we build with wood, hay and stubble, it might look impressive in this world, and receive much praise from man but it will not stand the test of the fire on the day of judgment. You might be thought of highly here, but on the last day there will be no reward for this work. It is sad to think of some ministers and others who worked hard and yet achieved nothing of lasting value. Their work was useless because it was man's ideas rather than following the direction of Scripture.

Reward is also meant to be an incentive to the Christian. Our great incentive is of course the cross. Paul states, 'For the love of Christ constraineth us' (2 Corinthians 5:14). But yet Christ encourages us, 'For whosoever shall give you a cup of water to drink in my name, because ye belong to Christ, verily I say unto you, he shall not lose his reward' (Mark

9:41). Paul himself states: 'I press toward the mark for the prize of the high calling of God in Christ Jesus' (Philippians 3:14). He wants his beloved Philippians to be richly rewarded: 'I desire fruit that may abound to your account' (Philippians 4:17). We are warned, 'Behold, I come quickly: hold that fast which thou hast, that no man take thy crown' (Revelation 3:11).

Will the sins of God's people be revealed?
When we become Christians all our sins are pardoned and washed away. If they were to be revealed on the judgment day, would that not be a form of punishment and leave us suffering and ashamed? Surely Christ has suffered for them and they are blotted out? We are told, 'As far as the east is from the west, so far hath he removed our transgressions from us' (Psalm 103:12). East and west will never meet so surely we will never meet our sins again? Yet we are told that the books shall be opened and we will be judged according to our works. Indeed Jesus warns his disciples, 'That every idle word that men shall speak, they shall give account thereof in the day of judgment' (Matthew 12:36). All our words are recorded. What a thought! There cannot be punishment for the Lord's people but all sins will be revealed and shown to be sins. This will not cause them grief but will encourage the song of the redeemed: 'Unto him that loved us, and washed us from our sins in his own blood, And hath made us kings and priests unto God and his Father; to him be glory and dominion for ever and ever. Amen' (Revelation 1:5-6). By this stage all Christians will be perfectly holy so there will be no room for pride, or boasting or envy. All Christians will be full of love to one another and to their Saviour.

You shall judge angels
Paul explains that Christians will have a role in the judgment: 'Do ye not know that the saints shall judge the world? and if the world shall be judged by you, are ye unworthy to judge the smallest matters? Know ye not that we shall judge angels? how much more things that pertain to this life?' (1 Corinthians 6:2-3). Christians in Corinth were falling out with one another and suing each other at law. Paul asks if there are no wise men among them

to whom they could go for judgment rather than take their disputes before the heathen. Surely it is better to suffer loss than allow such a terrible witness before the world? Somehow, Christians will join with Christ in the final judgment. They will even be involved in pronouncing sentence on angels.

Much is mysterious but some things are clear. We rejoice with the apostle who could say as his end approached: 'Henceforth there is laid up for me a crown of righteousness, which the Lord, the righteous judge, shall give me at that day: and not to me only, but unto all them also that love his appearing' (2 Timothy 4:8).

CHAPTER 9

HELL

No doctrine is more unpopular today than the biblical teaching concerning the everlasting punishment of unbelievers. Even evangelical churches are reluctant to proclaim that those who die unconverted will be cast into the lake of fire to be tormented forever. When liberalism came into the churches in the nineteenth century the doctrine of the universal fatherhood of God became very popular. This led in turn to the idea that because every man and woman was thought to be a child of God, therefore God could not possibly cast them, His children, into Hell forever. So from this arose the false doctrine of universalism, the idea that all will eventually be saved.

Up until the late nineteenth century it was recognised that only in a very general sense could God, as the Creator of all, be thought of as a parent to all. There are a few verses in Scripture which give some support to that idea. For example, Paul, preaching to the philosophers of Athens, quotes with approval a heathen poet who said, 'We are also his offspring' (Acts 17:28). This however was not seen as a father-child relationship, but simply that God was the creator and originator of man. The great emphasis of Scripture is quite different from the universal fatherhood of God. The Bible teaches that we only become God's children by adoption, 'Ye have received the Spirit of adoption, whereby we cry, Abba, Father' (Romans 8:15). You cannot adopt your own child. In another place Paul states, 'For ye are all the children of God by faith in Christ Jesus' (Galatians 3:26). From this we must deduce that unbelievers are not the children of God. Indeed, Jesus can say to the Jews, 'Ye are of your father the devil, and the lusts of your father ye will do' (John 8:44). As fallen children of Adam we are all born children of the devil and need to be converted and adopted to become the children of God and so to have the favour and everlasting love of our divine Father.

THE GLORIOUS FUTURE

Postmodernism
Postmodernism today is even more radical. Political correctness demands that we affirm everyone else's views. It is argued that everyone has his or her own truth. Postmodernism is totally against objective truth and the idea that there is only one way of salvation and that followers of other religions will perish. To assert such a view is in the eyes of the Postmodernists to be guilty of a hate crime. The idea is that whatever you believe is right for you, but you must not impose your views on others. There is no such thing as objective truth. Strangely these views have totally captured the popular mind and now these ideas have taken over the universities, the schools, the media and the government. This philosophy is used to promote and exalt all kinds of sexual immorality. Freedom to practise the various perversions condemned by the law of God in Scripture, is placed on the same level as ending slavery and racism. To speak of a judgment day or the punishment of sin is therefore extremely unpopular and sadly this spirit of the age has invaded the Christian church. Some prominent and respected evangelical theologians such as John Stott, J W Wenham, Philip E Hughes, and Clark Pinnock, have been affected to the extent that they have argued against the traditional doctrine of everlasting punishment. We shall return to this later.

Biblical words for Hell
In the Hebrew of the Old Testament there are two main words for Hell. First there is the word *Sheol*. It has several meanings and these must be determined by the context. It can refer to the grave, or to the state of the dead, or to the place of torment for the wicked. The other word is *Gehenna*. It is the place of punishment for sinners. Originally it meant the valley of the son of Hinnom. This valley was just outside Jerusalem and it was there that children were burnt in the worship of the heathen god Moloch. Good king Josiah desecrated this heathen shrine and turned it into the rubbish tip for the city. Fires burned there constantly destroying the rubbish and there also the worms fed upon the rotting remains of animals and food. Therefore, it presented a picture of Hell, the dunghill and rubbish tip of the world, a loathsome place where worms and fire will be constantly

feeding upon those rebels who end up there. In the Greek of the New Testament the word *Hades* is the equivalent of the Hebrew *Sheol*. It can refer to the grave or to the place where all go when they die, but more commonly is used for the place of eternal punishment for unbelievers.

Hell in the Old Testament

From the very beginning of Scripture, it was revealed that this life is not the end and that there is a judgment day and a Heaven and a Hell. We are told that 'Enoch walked with God: and he was not; for God took him' (Genesis 5:24). Others had died but Enoch went straight to Heaven to dwell with God. Jude tells us that Enoch prophesied, 'Behold the Lord cometh with ten thousands of his saints, To execute judgment upon all, and to convince all that are ungodly among them of all their ungodly deeds which they have ungodly committed, and of all their hard speeches which ungodly sinners have spoken against him' (Jude 14-15). We are assured by Jude that Enoch told these things to the ancient world. Even in these early days it was clear that the wicked would be punished.

David in the Psalms speaks of Hell as a place of punishment for the wicked: 'The Lord is known by the judgment which he executeth: the wicked is snared in the work of his own hands.... The wicked shall be turned into hell, and all the nations that forget God' (Psalm 9:16-17). The prophets also speak of Hell. Isaiah describes it in vivid terms: 'And they shall go forth, and look upon the carcases of the men that have transgressed against me: for their worm shall not die, neither shall their fire be quenched; and they shall be an abhorring unto all flesh' (Isaiah 66:24). These words are picked up by our Lord Jesus in describing the eternal misery of unbelievers and hypocrites: 'Where the worm dieth not, and the fire is not quenched' (Mark 9:48). Daniel prophesies concerning the resurrection that it will not simply be for the reward of the righteous but also for the punishment of the wicked: 'And many of them that sleep in the dust of the earth shall awake, some to everlasting life, and some to shame and everlasting contempt' (Daniel 12:2). Malachi further describes the punishment of unbelievers: 'For, behold, the day cometh, that shall burn as an oven; and all the proud, yea, and all that do wickedly, shall be stubble: and the day that cometh shall burn them up, saith the Lord of hosts, that it shall leave them neither root nor branch' (Malachi 4:1). Even in the Old Testament it is plain that those who die in their sins go to a place of conscious punishment.

Hell in the New Testament

No one speaks more about Hell than our loving Lord Jesus. He is concerned to warn men and women to flee from the wrath to come. He Himself suffered real Hell on the cross to deliver us from the Hell to come. He leaves us in no doubt that rejecting His gospel and His saving work at Calvary will not only result in one missing Heaven but will also cause that individual to be thrown into a Hell of everlasting misery.

In the Sermon on the Mount, Christ warns: 'And if thy right hand offend thee, cut it off, and cast it from thee: for it is profitable for thee that one of thy members should perish, and not that thy whole body should be cast into hell' (Matthew 5:30). If your hand is causing you to sin you should take drastic action. Hell is an awful place to end up in. Later, in the same sermon, Jesus reveals that there is a broad way that leads to eternal misery: 'Enter ye in at the strait gate: for wide is the gate, and broad is the way, that leadeth to destruction, and many there be which go in thereat' (Matthew 7:13).

Our Lord tells on another occasion the parable of the dragnet which captures good and bad fish. The fishermen then separate the edible fish from the useless. So it will be at the end of the world: 'The angels shall come forth, and sever the wicked from among the just, And shall cast them into the furnace of fire: there shall be wailing and gnashing of teeth' (Matthew 13:49-50). There is a place of great misery, of which Jesus spoke, where there will be weeping and grinding of teeth in pain. Who can imagine ending up in such a state? Similarly in the parable of the wedding feast, the command was given concerning the man who entered without a wedding garment, without the righteousness of Christ to clothe him, 'Bind him hand and foot, and take him away, and cast him into outer darkness, there shall be weeping and gnashing of teeth' (Matthew 22:13). On the judgment day which He explains is ahead of us all, it will be said to the unrighteous: 'Depart from me, ye cursed, into everlasting fire, prepared for the devil and his angels', and it is added, 'these shall go away into everlasting punishment: but the righteous into life eternal' (Matthew 25:41, 46). Mark records how Jesus spoke of some as being, 'cast into hell fire: where their worm dieth not, and the fire is not quenched' (Mark 9:47-48).

There can be no doubting that Jesus taught that there are two destinations in eternity. There is a Hell as well as a Heaven, and that Hell is a place of deep misery, of weeping and gnashing of teeth. It is a place of horrible pain with the worm gnawing and the fire burning. Now of course the worm and the fire are symbolic but they do convey the idea of extreme pain. Further this state is called 'everlasting punishment'. This suffering forever is the most awful aspect of it. There is no light at the end of the tunnel. There is no end of the pain and misery.

The Apostles also describe Hell in similar terms. Paul wrote of the coming of Christ: 'In flaming fire taking vengeance on them that know not God, and that obey not the gospel of our Lord Jesus Christ: who shall be punished with everlasting destruction from the presence of the Lord, and from the glory of his power' (2 Thessalonians 1:8-9). This is one great motive for Paul's preaching and missionary work: 'Knowing therefore the terror of the Lord, we persuade men' (2 Corinthians 5:11). Peter warns: 'The Lord knoweth how to deliver the godly out of temptations, and to reserve the unjust unto the day of judgment to be punished … But these, as natural brute beasts, made to be taken and destroyed, speak evil of the things that they understand not; and shall utterly perish in their own corruption … And shall receive the reward of unrighteousness … These are wells without water, clouds that are carried with a tempest; to whom the mist of darkness is reserved for ever' (2 Peter 2:9, 12, 13, 17).

The most graphic descriptions are to be found in the Book of Revelation where it is said of the wicked: 'The same shall drink of the wine of the wrath of God, which is poured out without mixture into the cup of his indignation; and he shall be tormented with fire and brimstone in the presence of the holy angels, and in the presence of the Lamb: and the smoke of their torment ascendeth up for ever and ever: and they have no rest day nor night, who worship the beast and his image, and whosoever receiveth the mark of his name' (Revelation 14:10-11). Later it is said, 'And whosoever was not found written in the book of life was cast into the lake of fire' (Revelation 20:15). There is the idea of exclusion from Heaven: 'For without are dogs, and sorcerers, and whoremongers, and murderers, and idolaters, and whosoever loveth and maketh a lie' (Revelation 22:15) and, so, missing the blessings of Heaven. But there is also the idea of positive punishment. Hell is described as a lake of fire. Few pains are as unbearable as burns. Here we are told that the 'smoke of their torment ascendeth up for ever and ever' (Revelation 14:11). The fire is unquenchable. It never goes out. 'They gnawed their tongues for pain' (Revelation 16:10). And it is a bottomless pit (Revelation 20:3) where there is a never-ending descending further and further into rebellion against God and blaspheming His name, and, so, experiencing more and more of His wrath.

Rejection of Hell

As we have shown this truth of everlasting conscious punishment of the wicked is the teaching of both the Old Testament and of the New Testament. This has been the traditional teaching of the church for the past 2000 years. However, with the growth of Higher Criticism which cast doubt on the inspiration and authority of Scripture, and liberalism denying the penal substitutionary atonement, doubts began to surface about Hell. How could a loving God punish huge numbers of men and women forever in Hell? Some, in response, have gone on to advocate universalism, the idea that every man and woman will eventually be saved.

There are two forms of this teaching. Some have advocated that there are many roads to God. This is *Pluralistic Universalism*. It teaches that all religions provide a way of salvation for their followers. Some get to Heaven through Islam and others through Hinduism. Humanists have their own path. This pluralism is directly contradicted by Christ who taught, 'I am the way, the truth, and the life: no man cometh unto the Father, but by me' (John 14:6). There is only one way to Heaven and that is through Christ.

The other form of Universalism is *Christian Universalism*. This position agrees that we can only be saved through Christ but argues that Christ atoned for the sin of the whole world, so, at the end of the day, the whole world will be saved through the mediatorial work of Christ. There are variations of this teaching with some speaking of a kind of purgatory after death when the individual is purified by some punishment which is endured. Traditional Roman Catholicism, of course, taught that there is a purgatory, but it is for baptised believers who are purified there, before going to Heaven. Purgatory of both kinds undermines the finished work of Christ who atoned for all His people's sins and only ascended up to Heaven when He had 'purged our sins' (Hebrews 1:3). But Roman Catholicism also believes in a Hell of everlasting suffering for the wicked.

Others who hold to a Christian Universalism assert that the unconverted will get a second chance to accept Christ as Saviour after death. Jesus however taught: 'Except a man be born again, he cannot see the kingdom of God' (John 3:3). He also taught that the rich man went straight to Hell when he died (Luke 16:23). In the parable of the Ten Virgins there was no second chance for those who had no oil with their lamps (Matthew 25:12). Jesus even warned respectable professing Christians when He said: 'Not every one that saith unto me, Lord, Lord, shall enter into the kingdom of heaven; but he that doeth the will of my Father which is in heaven. Many will say to me in that day, Lord, Lord, have we not prophesied in thy name? and in thy name have cast out devils? and in thy name done many wonderful works? And then will I profess unto them, I never knew you: depart from me, ye that work iniquity' (Matthew 7:21-23). From this it is plain that many will not be saved, even many church members, preachers and miracle workers. There is not a hint here of a second chance after death for those who die as unbelievers.

THE GLORIOUS FUTURE

Conditional Immortality

The false teaching of Conditional Immortality has recently become quite popular, supported by evangelical theologians such as John R. W. Stott, John W. Wenham, Philip E. Hughes, Edward William Fudge, and Clark H. Pinnock. It is the view that only true Christians will live forever and so experience everlasting life. Because they regard with abhorrence the idea of God forevermore, throughout the endless ages of eternity punishing men and women, they ask, how could a loving God ever do that? Does the Bible not say, 'God is love' (1 John 4:8, 16)? Surely this implies that love is the nature of God and so they argue that it is essential for God to show love to all men and women, or at the very least not to torment them forever.

This reasoning however forgets that God is not simply love. He is also truth, justice, wisdom, holiness and power. Just as the Scripture says that 'God is love,' it also says that 'God is a consuming fire' (Hebrews 12:29). That is terrifying but it would be a blessing to the church today if Christians and all mankind in general were aware of it and had more of the fear of God. Furthermore, when Scripture states that God is love it means that God is holy love and righteous love. Interestingly, in both the Old Testament and the New Testament, we find words of adoration, focusing specifically on the holiness of God. The Seraphim are seen in an awesome vision by Isaiah crying one to another, 'Holy, holy, holy, is the Lord of hosts: the whole earth is full of his glory' (Isaiah 6:3). We are told concerning the living creatures in John's vision of Heaven that, 'they rest not day and night, saying, Holy, holy, holy, Lord God Almighty, which was, and is, and is to come' (Revelation 4:8). Holiness, more than anything else, is revealed to us as distinctive of God. Nowhere in the Bible can the words be found, 'Love, love, love, is the Lord God Almighty,' though this too would be true of God. God is all His attributes. God is holy, God is just, God is true, God is wise and God is loving.

Sometimes it is even argued that it would be unjust for God to punish someone forever in Hell. Surely, they say, no sin committed in time could demand everlasting punishment. But what is forgotten is that sins against an infinitely good and loving God demand infinite and everlasting punishment. Also sinners in Hell go on blaspheming God and so deserve further punishment.

Exalting man as over against God
There is always a tendency of man to make God in his own image. Scripture lays particular emphasis on the holiness of God which is essentially the otherness of God. God's holiness is especially His majesty, His exaltedness, as well as His moral purity. Modern man thinks highly of himself and his own worth and his rights, and thinks little of the greatness and glory of God. Today's churches make God small and man big. It is because God is regarded as small that a sin against this kind of God is not seen as deserving eternal punishment. The Puritans rightly taught that even one sin against such a great and good God deserves eternal Hell. Sadly, all of us commit millions of sins in thought, word and deed against this God. The worst sin of all is rejecting the Saviour, the Son of God who came into this world and suffered so much to atone for our sins: 'How shall we escape, if we neglect so great salvation; which at the first began to be spoken by the Lord, and was confirmed unto us by them that heard him' (Hebrews 2:3). It was a wicked crime to crucify Him but it is an even worse crime to crucify Him a second time and that is the way unbelief is regarded in Scripture: 'they crucify to themselves the Son of God afresh, and put him to an open shame' (Hebrews 6:6). The writer to the Hebrews adds, 'He that despised Moses' law died without mercy under two or three witnesses: Of how much sorer punishment, suppose ye, shall he be thought worthy, who hath trodden under foot the Son of God, and hath counted the blood of the covenant, wherewith he was sanctified, an unholy thing, and hath done despite unto the Spirit of grace' (Hebrews 10:28-29). To ignore Christ and His work and the call to put our faith in Him, is regarded by God as a great insult and therefore worthy of the most awful punishment. It is because God is diminished and the work of Christ despised, while at the same time man is exalted, that modern theologians, reject the traditional idea of hell. Having reduced the truths of Scripture

to suit their own theories, they find the eternal, conscious punishment of human beings in the lake of fire, incredible and unacceptable.

Different forms of Conditional Immortality

There are different forms of this teaching of Conditional Immortality or as it is sometimes called, annihilationism. Some argue, for example, that all human beings are annihilated at death and only the saved are raised at the resurrection. This is the belief held by the Jehovah's Witnesses and Socinians and as we showed elsewhere is unbiblical. The more common form among many modern evangelicals who claim to follow the Bible, is that the conscious punishment of the wicked after death is temporary and then they will be annihilated. They argue that it is said in Scripture to be eternal because eventually the unbelievers are annihilated and so destroyed forever. Their experience of punishment is temporary but the punishment itself is eternal in that it ends their existence forever. Such theologians would take a verse like, 'Who shall be punished with everlasting destruction from the presence of the Lord' (2 Thessalonians 1:9) and reason that that destruction means complete destruction so that the wicked no longer exist. We will return to this matter later to show that while it could mean that, yet the rest of Scripture shows that this interpretation cannot be right.

God only is immortal

Some argue for Conditional Immortality on the basis that Scripture states that only God is immortal. Paul wrote of God as, 'The blessed and only Potentate, the King of kings, and Lord of lords; who only hath immortality, dwelling in the light which no man can approach unto; whom no man hath seen, nor can see: to whom be honour and power everlasting' (1 Timothy 6:15-16). God of course is indeed eternal and immortal in a way that no creature is. He had no beginning and will have no end. He is independent and self-existent and needs no one. Man has a beginning and is dependent on God every moment for his continued existence. Further, it is argued that eternal life is something which only believers attain. Scriptures such as the following are quoted, 'He that believeth on the Son hath everlasting life: and he that believeth not the Son shall not see life; but the wrath of God abideth on him' (John 3:36). From this it is stated that only those who believe in the Son of God have everlasting life. But in this verse everlasting life means life in Heaven. The existence of those in Hell is described as the second death. It is a constant dying, but yet complete death is impossible.

Considering that the church has always believed in the conscious experience of eternal punishment in Hell it is somewhat surprising to see how popular Conditional Immortality is becoming. John Stott was an Anglican evangelical who wrote many excellent books and was hugely influential amongst evangelical Christians across the world. It was therefore surprising when he questioned the everlasting nature of punishment in Hell in the book *Essentials: A Liberal-Evangelical Dialogue* (1988).

Hell is Eternal Conscious Suffering

Hell is eternal, conscious suffering. This is revealed in a number of biblical passages. Jesus speaks of a place of 'weeping and gnashing of teeth' (Matthew 22:13). This involves ongoing suffering. He further describes Hell as a place where there is fire that never shall be quenched: 'where their worm dieth not, and the fire is not quenched' (Mark 9:44). If Hell is a place where there is fire that is never quenched, it obviously needs fuel, something to burn forever. The worm will die if it has nothing to feed on. The whole idea of fire that is never quenched necessitates ongoing existence for the wicked, and similarly the undying worm. The judgment is portrayed for us in Matthew 25. The final statement there of Christ with regard to the punishment of the wicked is that it is eternal, 'These shall go away into everlasting punishment: but the righteous into life eternal' (v46). In the Greek original the same word *aioneon* is used to describe the eternity of the life of the righteous and the eternity of the suffering of the wicked. If eternal life goes on forever and Heaven is everlasting conscious enjoyment of God then Hell must be everlasting conscioius punishment by God.

There is no end envisioned in the Hell to which the rich man went: 'And in hell he lift up his eyes, being in torments, and seeth Abraham afar off, and Lazarus in his bosom. And he cried and said, Father Abraham, have mercy on me, and send Lazarus, that he may dip the tip of his finger in water, and cool my tongue; for I am tormented in this flame … but Abraham said … beside all this, between us and you there is a great gulf fixed: so that they which would pass from hence to you cannot; neither can they pass to us, that would come from thence' (Luke 16:23-26). There is no second chance. There is no way from Heaven to Hell and none who go to Hell will ever get to Heaven. The great gulf between the two cannot be bridged.

The Book of Revelation describes the endlessness of Hell: 'And the devil that deceived them was cast into the lake of fire and brimstone, where the beast and the false prophet are, and shall be tormented day and night for ever and ever' (Revelation 20:10). And then it is stated, 'And whosoever was not found written in the book of life was cast into the lake of fire' (v15). Earlier in the book we are told with regard to the wicked, 'The same shall drink of the wine of the wrath of God, which is poured out without mixture into the cup of his indignation; and he shall be tormented with fire and brimstone in the presence of the holy angels, and in the presence of the Lamb' (Revelation 14:10). Surely that means never-ending suffering?

Sometimes it is argued that the existence of Hell would be a blot on God's universe forever. How could God allow that there should be a place of blasphemy and rebellion and suffering throughout eternity? What is often forgotten in this type of reasoning is that God will be glorified in the destruction of the wicked just as He is glorified in the salvation of the saints. God glorifies His mercy, love and wisdom in saving sinners. God also glorifies and displays His justice and wrath in punishing the wicked forever. Hell will be a constant reminder to the people of God what our Saviour endured for us and what He saved us from. This will take nothing away from our eternal songs of praise but rather add to them.

One problem many have is how they could possibly be happy in Heaven thinking of their family suffering in Hell. What about a loving parent, a dear spouse, a child who is precious to us? It is indeed hard for us to envisage ourselves being content while they are being punished.

However, on the judgment day we will see the true wickedness of the unbeliever as we have never seen it in this life. We will know even as we are known (1 Corinthians 13:12). We will have such love and admiration for God that we will acquiesce fully in His judgment.

Chapter 10

HEAVEN

Having dealt with the eternal state of the wicked we now come to consider the everlasting bliss which lies ahead of the righteous. The great Judge will say to the unbelievers, 'Depart from me, ye cursed', but He will say to those who trust in Him, 'Come, ye blessed of my Father, inherit the kingdom prepared for you from the foundation of the world' (Matthew 25:34). How awful is that word 'Depart', depart forever, but how wonderful is the word 'Come', come and dwell with Me forever! Christ had comforted His disciples as He was about to leave them the night before He was crucified: 'Let not your heart be troubled: ye believe in God, believe also in me. In my Father's house are many mansions: if it were not so, I would have told you. I go to prepare a place for you. And if I go and prepare a place for you, I will come again, and receive you unto myself; that where I am, there ye may be also' (John 14:1-3). But what will this Heaven, this house of many mansions be like? This is the subject we would like to deal with in this final chapter.

Just as with Hell, the pictures and symbolism of Heaven presented to us are in graphic and metaphorical terms. None of us has been there and therefore we have difficulty picturing it. It will be very different from our present state. In many ways, the best we can say is in negative terms, contrasting Heaven with the troubles and sufferings of the present time. We know that it will be very good and the best that the Almighty, the all-wise God can give to us. God knows us, and He knows how to make us really happy. He created us to glorify and enjoy Him. In this world, because of the Fall, even when we wish to fulfil the purpose for which we were created, we often fail miserably, but in Heaven we will succeed perfectly. All the sin and misery which characterised the state into which we fell in Adam, shall be gone forever. Even in this life, we who have been born again, from time to time enjoy moments of felt fellowship with God and to us they are, as it were, Heaven on earth. In this way already we experience 'joy unspeakable and full of glory' (1 Peter 1:8). If those moments are so sweet, how wonderful Heaven will be!

Where will Heaven be?

Where will Heaven be located? There is clearly a place, distinct from this world, where Heaven is at the moment. We are told that Enoch and Elijah went bodily to Heaven, so there must be a physical place where they are living. Our Lord Jesus, on the fortieth day after His resurrection, ascended up to Heaven while the disciples watched, and a cloud received Him out of their sight. He too is living bodily in the location which the Bible calls Heaven. Two angels then appeared to the disciples and said, 'Ye men of Galilee, why stand ye gazing up into heaven? this same Jesus, which is taken up from you into heaven, shall so come in like manner as ye have seen him go into heaven' (Acts 1:11). At the present time, therefore, there is a place distinct from this earth and it is called Heaven. God is omnipresent, yet He is especially present in Heaven. This is the dwelling place of the angels who, although they do not have bodies, are not infinite like God, but spatially limited. They can only be in one place at one time. Here also the souls of the saints who have died, dwell with their Saviour. It is described as being above us and yet it is not somewhere that can be reached by a space rocket.

At the same time, heaven cannot be very far away, because Saul of Tarsus could see clearly into it from the Damascus Road, seeing the man Christ Jesus and speaking to Him: 'And he said, Who art thou, Lord? And the Lord said, I am Jesus whom thou persecutest: it is hard for thee to kick against the pricks. And he trembling and astonished said, Lord, what wilt thou have me to do? And the Lord said unto him, Arise, and go into the city, and it shall be told thee what thou must do' (Acts 9:5-6). Heaven, it would seem, is in a kind of parallel universe, not that far away and yet impossible to see with a human telescope. It is interesting how Jesus could appear and disappear after His resurrection.

THE GLORIOUS FUTURE

John's Vision of Heaven

Following his vision of the judgment day, the Apostle John is given a revelation of Heaven. He tells us what he saw: 'I saw a new heaven and a new earth: for the first heaven and the first earth were passed away; and there was no more sea' (Revelation 21:1). The old heaven and earth is the universe which we now inhabit. It has many beautiful spots – mountains, forests, lakes, beaches and gardens. We have happy memories of delightful places. But there are also thorns and thistles, diseases and plagues, storms and disasters, wars and famines. But Heaven is a new world where everything is beautiful, healthy, full of life and very good.

John tells how he saw the church descending to earth: 'And I John saw the holy city, new Jerusalem, coming down from God out of heaven, prepared as a bride adorned for her husband' (Revelation 21:2). Some have argued that the present universe will pass out of existence and Heaven will be a totally new and unconnected place. This, however, seems unlikely. God created a beautiful and wonderful world in the beginning and Satan destroyed it. It is certain that Satan will not have the ultimate victory. When the ancient world came under God's judgment it was destroyed with a flood and a purified world arose from under the flood waters. The present world will be destroyed with fire: 'But the heavens and the earth, which are now, by the same word are kept in store, reserved unto fire against the day of judgment and perdition of ungodly men' (2 Peter 3:7). Peter adds, 'The heavens shall pass away with a great noise, and the elements shall melt with fervent heat, the earth also and the works that are therein shall be burned up. Seeing then that all these things shall be dissolved, what manner of persons ought ye to be in all holy conversation and godliness, looking for and hasting unto the coming of the day of God, wherein the heavens being on fire shall be dissolved, and the elements shall melt with fervent heat?' (vv10-12). From this massive conflagration a new world will emerge, a new heavens and earth. But the new will have continuity with the old. Just as the body of the saint is buried in the earth a natural and corruptible body, but rises from the grave incorruptible, immortal and perfectly suited for eternity, so it will be with the new earth.

HEAVEN

This 'restitution of all things' (Acts 3:21) spoken of by Peter, the Apostle Paul anticipated in the following way: 'For we know that the whole creation groaneth and travaileth in pain together until now. And not only they, but ourselves also, which have the firstfruits of the Spirit, even we ourselves groan within ourselves, waiting for the adoption, to wit, the redemption of our body' (Romans 8:22-23). The world around us is pictured as writhing in agony because of the curse of God which sin brought upon it. Earthquakes, tsunamis, volcanoes, and hurricanes show a world in pain. This world is personified as longing for redemption. One day the heavens and the earth which are now, will be regenerated and become the new heavens and earth. This will take place alongside the resurrection of the saints, their bodies redeemed as well as their souls and their status as the adopted children of God demonstrated. Heaven will be a restored and greatly improved Garden of Eden where sin and Satan shall never again enter to destroy.

God's Presence

John describes the special presence of God enjoyed by those who are saved: 'And I heard a great voice out of heaven saying, Behold, the tabernacle of God is with men, and he will dwell with them, and they shall be his people, and God himself shall be with them, and be their God' (Revelation 21:3). In a very real sense God's presence was with Israel as they journeyed through the wilderness. The pillar of cloud by day and the pillar of fire by night led them. God's presence was in the Holy of Holies in the tabernacle and, later, in the temple, sitting on the mercy-seat above the ark of the covenant. But from time to time God was grieved with their sin and withdrew. Also there was the veil of the tabernacle which separated even the priests from God. But in the New Jerusalem, God pitches His tent among His people and the veil has been torn down. The saints will have constant and enjoyable access to God.

Moses, on one occasion, pleaded with God, 'I beseech thee, show me thy glory' (Exodus 33:18). God placed him in a cleft of a rock and, as it were, placed His hand over him and then passed by so that Moses was able to see the back parts of God. God is a Spirit and has no body, but something of the glory of God was revealed to Moses. Paul explains the future knowledge of God's people: 'For now we see through a glass, darkly; but then face to face: now I know in part; but then shall I know even as also I am known' (1 Corinthians 13:12). John in his epistle asserts: 'Beloved, now are we the sons of God, and it doth not yet appear what we shall be: but we know that, when he shall appear, we shall be like him; for we shall see him as he is' (1 John 3:2). One day we will see God and be transformed into His likeness and not just get a glimpse but fill our eyes and our hearts with the beatific vision.

Every human being, as someone said, has a God-shaped hole in their heart. As Augustine put it, 'Thou hast made us for thyself and our hearts are restless till they find their rest in thee'. We need God, we seek God and in heaven we fully find Him. God makes a great promise to those who reach heaven: 'They shall be his people, and God himself shall be with them, and be their God' (Revelation 21:3). God of course has already made His covenant with us and entered into a huge commitment. He has already revealed Himself to us and we have by grace embraced Him. He is our God and undertakes to do everything a God can do for us. We commit ourselves to Him, trusting Him and giving our hearts and lives to Him. In Heaven, however, we will fully and forever experience God. In this world we sometimes grow spiritually cold. We backslide and are caught up with the cares and pleasures of the world and because of this, God in His divine displeasure chastises us by removing from us the felt presence of Himself. But in Heaven we dwell in His presence. No sin can disturb our relationship with Him and we are satisfied with Him.

The New Jerusalem

Sometimes Heaven is described as a city, the new Jerusalem. It is not a lonely or desolate place. This life is often a waste, howling wilderness, but then, all that will be behind us. There are many lonely people in this world. Sometimes God's people can be neglectful of the chronically ill or elderly who are confined to their homes, but all who get to Heaven will have company and the very best company. It is a city inhabited by millions from every tribe and nation and tongue. It is God's house of many mansions with plenty of room. We are going home to be with our Father and the redeemed family.

Other times Heaven is described as a garden: 'And he shewed me a pure river of water of life, clear as crystal, proceeding out of the throne of God and of the Lamb. In the midst of the street of it, and on either side of the river, was there the tree of life, which bare twelve manner of fruits, and yielded her fruit every month: and the leaves of the tree were for the healing of the nations' (Revelation 22:1-2). It is the new Eden, a paradise garden of trees and flowers and a river running through it with crystal-clear water. This river of the water of life proceeds from the throne of God and of the Lamb. God, who is the sovereign Planner, will be the source of the life of all the men and women who get to heaven. Because the river is also expressed as flowing from the throne of the Lamb, we can see that the eternal life we will enjoy has been earned for us by Christ through His atoning death on the cross. From the throne of the loving God and the suffering Saviour, the Spirit flows to us as the life-giving, refreshing water. The Spirit beautifies the garden and fills the children of God with eternal joy. Just as in Eden there was the tree of life so here Christ is to us the tree of life. God's people have unrestricted access to its nourishing and varied fruits and its leaves are for the healing of the nations. Christ is the very centre of Paradise, and it is His presence that makes Heaven, Heaven to His people: 'For the Lamb which is in the midst of the throne shall feed them, and shall lead them unto living fountains of waters' (Revelation 7:17).

No suffering

In this life there is much pain and suffering but in Heaven we are told, 'God shall wipe away all tears from their eyes; and there shall be no more death, neither sorrow, nor crying, neither shall there be any more pain: for the former things are passed away' (Revelation 21:4). This life can be described as a vale of tears. We enter it with a cry and often leave it also with a cry.

There are tears due to physical pain, to psychological pain, to unkindness from those around us, to grief and to bereavement. But in Heaven, God wipes away all tears. Many tears are shed in sorrow over sin, but now all our sins are washed away and we will never sin again and so, joyfully we sing, 'Unto him that loved us, and washed us from our sins in his own blood' (Revelation 1:5).

There will be no more death. This is a huge part of the curse which came on mankind because of sin: 'Dust thou art, and unto dust shalt thou return' (Genesis 3:19). The ageing process began when Adam sinned. Man is subject to all kinds of horrible illnesses and diseases. In the ancient world leprosy was dreaded. Today it is cancer. But in Heaven there is no illness, weakness or disability. All which in this world leads to misery and death has been removed. There will be 'no more pain'. What a wonderful truth this is! Some godly people know much pain and weakness in this life and struggle long with disability. Many know terrible suffering from mental illness, depression and anxiety. These former things have now passed away. 'And there shall be no more curse' (Revelation 22:3).

No Sin

One of the things God's children most look forward to about Heaven is the end of sinning: 'His servants shall serve him: And they shall see his face; and his name shall be in their foreheads' (Revelation 22:3-4). Because we love God, we hate sin. We are constantly battling against temptation, against the world, the flesh and the devil. When we are converted we die to sin as our master. It no longer has dominion over us (Romans 6:14), but it is still constantly troubling us. As long as we are in this life, sin is sadly very easy and natural for us. We are troubled with anger, lust, covetousness, hypocrisy and pride. Cares and pleasures readily become gods to us. We long to be perfectly holy and pleasing to God. It is wonderful to look forward to a Heaven where God is on the throne in our hearts and self is completely subordinate to our Lord. Thankfully in Heaven there is no devil. Satan and his demons will be locked up in the bottomless pit. The ungodly world will also be cast into Hell. The 'flesh' will not enter Heaven.

Nothing unclean will be there. How hard it is for us to control our sinful thoughts and filthy lusts, but in Heaven these will be a thing of the past. Our hearts' desire is to worship God without distraction and to serve Him without pride intruding. We long to be like Him and one day soon we will be so like Him as that we will have His name on our foreheads.

No night there
We are told, 'there shall be no night there' (Revelation 22:5). There will be no darkness in Heaven and no works of darkness: 'God is light, and in him is no darkness at all' (1 John 1:5). There will be no sun or moon. There is no need for such: 'And the city had no need of the sun, neither of the moon, to shine in it: for the glory of God did lighten it, and the Lamb is the light thereof. And the nations of them which are saved shall walk in the light of it: and the kings of the earth do bring their glory and honour into it' (Revelation 21:23-24). Hell is outer darkness and the 'blackness of darkness forever' (Jude 13) but Heaven is full of light. Night is the time of tiredness but there will be no weariness or exhaustion in Heaven. Night is the time when thieves and robbers do their work but there will be no criminals in Heaven. Wild animals hunt in the darkness but in Heaven there will be nothing to attack us. Night is a time of fear but there will be no fear in Heaven. The prince of darkness delights in coming in the night, disturbing our sleep, bringing waves of anxiety, but there will be no night there. Nights can be times of weeping, but 'joy cometh in the morning' (Psalm 30:5). Heaven will be one everlasting morning of joy.

No more sea
The Apostle John states that 'There was no more sea' (Revelation 21:1). This is initially surprising to us. Many of us enjoy going to the seaside, viewing the cliffs, the rocks, the sandy beaches. We love to sail on the sea and to fish. The sea has great beauty whether calm or stormy. But for John the sea meant imprisonment. He tells us he was on the Isle of Patmos a prisoner 'for the word of God, and for the testimony of Jesus Christ' (Revelation 1:9). He would stand on the shore of his island prison and look

across to the mainland towards his beloved Ephesus and think of his Christian brothers and sisters and long to have fellowship with them and minister to them. The sea separated him from the church. He looked forward to the day when there would be no more sea of separation from fellow-Christians, but unity and fellowship for evermore. Others as they look at the sea, think of loved ones lost in storms. The Apostle Paul himself suffered shipwreck four times. On one occasion, he tells that he spent a night and a day in the deep (2 Corinthians 11:25) and after writing that epistle, as a prisoner on his way to Rome, he suffered another shipwreck following a terrifying storm that lasted many days, but in answer to prayer he landed on Malta. How many lives has the sea devoured over the years, but 'the sea gave up the dead which are in it' (Revelation 20:13) and now there shall be no more sea.

The glory of the City

In Revelation 21 there is a lengthy description of the city, New Jerusalem. It is a great city (Revelation 21:10) which will be required to house the innumerable crowd saved by the blood of Christ. Abraham was assured that his children would be as the stars of Heaven and as the sand by the sea shore for multitude (Genesis 15:5; 22:17). It is a holy city (v10). Nothing sinful will enter Heaven: 'And there shall in no wise enter into it any thing that defileth, neither whatsoever worketh abomination, or maketh a lie: but they which are written in the Lamb's book of life' (Revelation 21:27). It is further said that outside, 'are dogs, and sorcerers, and whoremongers, and murderers, and idolaters, and whosoever loveth and maketh a lie' (Revelation 22:15). The only ones who enter Heaven are those who are washed in the blood of Christ, justified and sanctified: 'These are they which came out of great tribulation, and have washed their robes, and made them white in the blood of the Lamb. Therefore are they before the throne of God, and serve him day and night in his temple: and he that sitteth on the throne shall dwell among them. They shall hunger no more, neither thirst any more; neither shall the sun light on them, nor any heat' (Revelation 7:14-16).

HEAVEN

The New Jerusalem has the glory of God and symbolically is like a precious jasper stone clear as crystal (Revelation 21:11). Heaven is made of jewels, the gates are of pearls and the streets of gold. We are told that it is made of the most precious things we know. Gold, for which many sell their souls, is as common as the dust under the feet of those in Heaven. The wall is great and high because it is a great city. There are twelve gates, facing in all directions. The gates are open welcoming all who will receive the gospel and come. But the gospel must be accepted in this life because 'it is appointed unto men once to die, but after this the judgment' (Hebrews 9:27). Once death comes there is no second chance. Death is followed by judgment.

The walls of the city have twelve foundations in which are written the names of the twelve apostles. The church is built on 'the foundation of the apostles and prophets, Jesus Christ himself being the chief corner stone' (Ephesians 2:20). The apostles had a vitally important role in organising the church and in revealing the truth. The perfection of the city is further emphasised in that it is a cube, the length, the breadth and the height of it being equal. The length, breadth and height are twelve thousand furlongs. The number twelve is significant. It is three times four, three for the Trinity and four for the four corners of the earth. The thousand emphasises its greatness. We have here the Trinity working for the salvation of the earth. The different foundations are of different precious stones and so truly magnificent.

There was no Temple there

Because temples and churches are so important to God's people in this world we are surprised by the fact that there is no temple in the New Jerusalem. But what we must remember is that it is all temple. Many compare the Garden of Eden to a temple but how much more Heaven is a temple. The throne of God and the Lamb is central. All the inhabitants are pictured surrounding the throne. We think of John's first vision into Heaven: 'Behold, a throne was set in heaven, and one sat on the throne. And he that sat was to look upon like a jasper and a sardine stone: and there was a rainbow round about the throne, in sight like unto an emerald. And round about the throne were four and twenty seats: and upon the seats I saw four and twenty elders sitting, clothed in white raiment; and they had on their heads crowns of gold' (Revelation 4:2-4). The twenty-four elders represent the church in the Old Testament and the New Testament. Then we are told of the worship: 'The four and twenty elders fall down before him that sat on the throne, and worship him that liveth for ever and ever, and cast their crowns before the throne, saying, Thou art worthy, O Lord, to receive glory and honour and power: for thou hast created all things, and for thy pleasure they are and were created' (v10-11). The four living creatures who were before the throne, 'Rest not day and night, saying, Holy, holy, holy, Lord God Almighty, which was, and is, and is to come' (v8). The glory of the nations is prostrated at the feet of King Jesus: 'They shall bring the glory and honour of the nations into it' (Revelation 21:26).

Will we know one another in Heaven?

Sometimes the question is asked, Will we know one another in Heaven? It would seem very strange if we did not. Surely, we will not be more ignorant then than we are now! When Moses and Elijah appeared on the mount of transfiguration, they did not require an introduction to the disciples to tell who they were. The rich man in Hell looking up to Heaven immediately recognised his father Abraham. However, Jesus makes plain that family relationships will not exist as they do on earth. The Sadducees asked Him concerning a woman who had had in turn seven brothers as her husbands. Whose wife would she be in Heaven? Jesus states clearly that the Sadducees err, not knowing the Scripture, 'For in the resurrection they neither marry, nor are given in marriage, but are as the angels of God in heaven' (Matthew 22:30). There will be no family groups neither will there be special parties or cliques. All will be the children of God and all will be united in perfect love one for another.

How will we view loved ones in Hell?

One matter which perplexes many is how we will view loved ones in Hell. We touched on this at the end of the previous chapter. The thought of a child or a spouse, or parent, or sibling ending up in Hell is hard for us to accept. We love our friends and family and hate to see them suffer. Would the lostness of someone precious to us, spoil our Heaven? What we must realise is that nothing will spoil Heaven. The judgment day will demonstrate the wickedness of the wicked and the justice of God. In this life we have little understanding of the evil of sin and particularly how wrong it is to reject or even ignore the call of the gospel. Christ suffered immense pain to save us and offered salvation to all. To reject Christ and, as it were, to trample His blood underfoot, deserves great punishment. Our love being first and foremost to God will mean that we will fully and happily acquiesce in His judgment.

Occupation in Heaven

What will our occupation be in Heaven? Some think that our occupations may be similar to what they are in this life but without sin. We cannot be sure. Certainly, we will be praising and giving thanks to God. Will we get bored? Definitely not! God knows what is best and He will design a Heaven which suits His people and makes them completely happy. Central to it all will be the worship of God.

Just as in Hell the punishments vary according to privileges and sins, so the rewards in Heaven will vary according to faithfulness, love to the Saviour, diligence in labours for the Master and holiness of life, but all will be fully satisfied. God is infinitely great and so a central part of Heaven will be discovering more and more about God and praising Him accordingly.

Heaven is described as the marriage supper of the Lamb. The bride has made herself ready, and 'She shall be brought unto the king in raiment of needlework: the virgins her companions that follow her shall be brought unto thee. With gladness and rejoicing shall they be brought: they shall enter into the king's palace' (Psalm 45:14-15). The garment of needlework is the holiness of the saints. The church will forever be married to Christ and enjoy His company to all eternity: 'For the Lamb which is in the midst of the throne shall feed them' (Revelation 7:17). It will be a feast of love, Christ loving us, and we loving Him, delighting in Him, and feeding upon Him forever.

THE AUTHOR

REV WILLIAM MACLEOD, BSc, ThM, a retired Free Church of Scotland (Continuing) minister, was brought up in Stornoway, Isle of Lewis. After studies at the Free Church College, Edinburgh, and Westminster Theological Seminary in the USA, he became minister of the Partick Free Church (Glasgow) congregation in 1976. He was translated to Portree (Isle of Skye) in 1993 and then to Thornwood (now Knightswood) (Glasgow) in 2006, retiring in 2021. He was Moderator of the General Assembly of the Free Church of Scotland (Continuing) in 2005, 2019 & 2020, Principal of the Free Church (Continuing) Seminary from 2002-14 and lecturer in Systematic Theology from 2017-21. He was also Editor of the Church's magazine, the *Free Church Witness*, between 2000 and 2017. He is married to Marion and they have three adult children.

THE GLORIOUS FUTURE